AFRICAN ETHNOGRAPHIC STUDIES
OF THE 20TH CENTURY

Volume 36

THE PASTORAL FULBE FAMILY
IN GWANDU

THE PASTORAL FULBE FAMILY IN GWANDU

C. EDWARD HOPEN

R Routledge
Taylor & Francis Group

LONDON AND NEW YORK

First published in 1958 by Oxford University Press for the International African Institute.

This edition first published in 2018
by Routledge
2 Park Square, Milton Park, Abingdon, Oxon OX14 4RN

and by Routledge
711 Third Avenue, New York, NY 10017

Routledge is an imprint of the Taylor & Francis Group, an informa business

British Library Cataloguing in Publication Data
A catalogue record for this book is available from the British Library

ISBN: 978-0-8153-8713-8 (Set)
ISBN: 978-0-429-48813-9 (Set) (ebk)
ISBN: 978-1-138-59431-9 (Volume 36) (hbk)
ISBN: 978-1-138-59433-3 (Volume 36) (pbk)
ISBN: 978-0-429-48895-5 (Volume 36) (ebk)

Publisher's Note
The publisher has gone to great lengths to ensure the quality of this reprint but points out that some imperfections in the original copies may be apparent.

Disclaimer
The publisher has made every effort to trace copyright holders and would welcome correspondence from those they have been unable to trace.

THE PASTORAL
FULBE FAMILY
IN GWANDU

BY

C. EDWARD HOPEN

Published for the
INTERNATIONAL AFRICAN INSTITUTE
by the
OXFORD UNIVERSITY PRESS
LONDON IBADAN ACCRA
1958

Oxford University Press, Amen House, London E.C.4

GLASGOW   NEW YORK   TORONTO   MELBOURNE   WELLINGTON
BOMBAY   CALCUTTA   MADRAS   KARACHI   KUALA LUMPUR
CAPE TOWN   IBADAN   NAIROBI   ACCRA

PRINTED IN GREAT BRITAIN

FOREWORD

D ISPERSED in a number of scattered clusters over a zone of
more than 2,000 miles, extending from Senegal to beyond
Lake Chad, in the interior of West Africa, live a series of
ethnically related peoples who, distinguished by their speech,
appearance, and pastoral traditions, have long been set apart from
the farming populations of the villages and towns of the Western
Sudan. Calling themselves Fulɓe and more commonly known in
Northern Nigeria by the local Hausa term 'Fulani', several of these
groups have played a remarkable part in the economic life and
political history of the chiefdoms and empires of the region. In
particular, a Fulani-led Holy War (*Jihad*) at the beginning of the
nineteenth century established their dominion over Hausa and
other chiefdoms in what is now Northern Nigeria, and it was with
a Fulani governing aristocracy that the British authorities had to
deal when the Protectorate was established a hundred years later.

By that time the Fulani rulers of the chiefdoms had, for the most
part, lost their pastoral traditions, but their cattle-herding con-
geners still migrated seasonally on the confines of the village lands.
Indeed, the pacification and the later economic changes offered the
pastoralists new opportunities to extend their migrations in search
of pasture. Still more recently, the future role of the pastoral
Fulani in the developing economy of Northern Nigeria has become
a subject of increasingly urgent consideration. And similar problems concerning these cattle people have presented themselves
in other parts of West Africa.

Yet, despite the intrinsic interest attaching to their way of life,
the significant part their forebears had played in the political scene,
and the practical needs and opportunities presented by their
economy, surprisingly little systematic knowledge had until
recently been gained concerning the material and social conditions
of pastoral life in West Africa, or the factors underlying the tenacity
with which the pastoral Fulani have maintained their ethnic and
social separateness. Some external aspects of their life, the appearance of their camps, their herding practices, and the character of
their more conspicuous ceremonies have been described, but the
particular values and motives, the ecological and social pressures
and rewards which sustained the herding household and camp

group, and determined the seasonal movements of fluctuating encampments, remained mainly a matter of surmise. This ignorance
resulted in large measure from the special difficulties involved in
any attempt to establish intimate contact with migrating households
and close observation of short-lived camp groups.

Recognizing the scientific and practical need to gain greater
knowledge of the ecology and social life of these peoples, to ascer-
tain the main variants in their patterns of seasonal migration and
the degree to which, under differing conditions, they combined
cattle-rearing with cultivation, the Council of the International
African Institute some years ago approved a proposal to encourage
intensive field studies among the pastoral Fulani in different parts
of West Africa. It was fortunate in securing the assistance of the
Rockefeller Foundation in financing one such study for which
Mr. C. E. Hopen, the author of the present work, was appointed
to a Research Fellowship. This enabled him to live and work
among the pastoral Fulani of Gwandu Emirate in Northern Nigeria
for two periods in 1952–3 and 1953–5. At the same time, Dr. D. J.
Stenning, then a Goldsmith's Student of the University of Cam-
bridge, undertook a field study of pastoral Fulani in West Bornu,
and Mlle Dupire, attached to the Institut Français d'Afrique
Noire, carried out similar investigations in the Niger Province of
French West Africa and in the French Cameroons. In 1952, at an
early stage in their field inquiries, the Institute arranged for a
meeting of these research workers at Jos to enable them to exchange
information and ideas on the development of their several re-
searches and to take advantage of the long experience among the
Fulani of Mr. F. W. de St. Croix of the Nigerian Veterinary Ser-
vice, who kindly participated in their discussions.

It can confidently be anticipated that, as a result of these recent
field studies, a number of scholarly accounts of various aspects of
the culture and social life of several groups of pastoral Fulani will be
forthcoming, which will enable social anthropologists, West African administrators, development officers and others to appraise the
varying character and conditions of their economy and to gain a
deeper understanding of their social life.

In the present study Mr. Hopen is mainly concerned to show in
detail the interdependence of the family and its herd among the
pastoral Fulani of Gwandu. But since the ecological and cultural
setting of the Fulani household is both variable and unfamiliar, and

since, as he shows, the economic and political conditions of the pastoralists have changed both internally and in relation to the wider community of the Hausa districts and Fulani emirates, he has prefaced this study of Fulani domestic economy with an account, derived in large measure from the traditions of the groups with which he lived, of the part played by pastoral Fulani in the political life of what is now Northern Nigeria and of the changes in their own fortunes that have flowed from the rise of the Fulani Empire, its later dissensions, and its pacification and control under a British protectorate. Against this background the reader will better appreciate both the extent to which the social context of pastoral life has been modified in response to recent conditions, and also the degree to which the particular code of obligation to one another and aloofness from other people, connoted by the term Fulfulde, has been sustained and has preserved in so great a measure the distinctiveness, exclusiveness, and self-reliance with which the pastoral Fulani still today impress the other peoples among whom they move.

DARYLL FORDE

International African Institute
July 1957

In referring to vernacular words in the text, the following abbreviations have been used:

> H. = Hausa
> F. = Fulani
> Ar. = Arabic

ACKNOWLEDGEMENTS

THE Author wishes to express his very sincere thanks to all those whose kindness and courtesy so materially assisted him in carrying out his research. Particular mention should be made of the Administration of the Northern Region, Nigeria, and the Administration of Sokoto Province; Dr. Louis González and Dr. and Mrs. Andrew Currie of the Medical Department, Sokoto Province; Mr. de St. Croix, for his advice both before and during the field study; the staff of the West African Institute of Social and Economic Research, Ibadan; the Rockefeller Foundation of New York, whose generosity enabled the research to be carried out; Dr. D. J. Stenning for reading this report in draft and for many helpful suggestions; the Central Research Fund of the University of London for the loan of photographic equipment and for a grant; and numerous Fulani informants whose interest and co-operation made this research not only possible but pleasurable. In addition, thanks are due and are most gratefully offered to the International African Institute for planning and organizing the project and to Professor Daryll Forde, Director of the Institute, who supervised the work and whose constant assistance and advice, both in the course of the field study and during the preparation of this report, are most gratefully recognized.

CONTENTS

ILLUSTRATIONS

LIST OF MAPS

SECTION I

1

SIGNIFICANT ETHNIC AND SUB-CULTURAL DIVISIONS

THE Fulani[1] who are the subject of this study refer to themselves as *Fulɓe* (s. *Pullo*) and to their language as *Fulfulde*. To distinguish themselves from other Fulani, as they do in certain political and social contexts, they speak of themselves as *Fulɓe na'i* (cattle *Fulɓe*) or *Fulɓe ladɗe* (bush *Fulɓe*). The distinction has an ecological and a cultural basis, for in these respects they differ markedly from certain other peoples, all of whom are referred to by English-speaking scholars and observers as 'Fulani'. Thus, in speaking of themselves as *Fulɓe na'i* they distinguish themselves from the local non-pastoral, aristocratic ruling 'clan', the *Torooɓe* (see 'History and Traditions of Origin', p. 6), to whom they generally refer by their clan name. Less frequently the *Torooɓe* may also be called 'town *Fulɓe*' (*Fulɓe siire*, H. *Fulanin gida*), but as a rule the latter term is restricted in reference to erstwhile pastoralists who have permanently lost their cattle through disease or poor husbandry and have been forced to adopt the mode of livelihood of the Hausa-speaking peasantry. Today the *Torooɓe* do not speak *Fulfulde* and, in physical appearance, they closely resemble the non-Fulani Hausa-speakers among whom they live. On the other hand, the *Fulɓe siire* may or may not speak the Fulani language, depending on the scale of their local settlement among non-Fulani, and the length of time elapsed since they gave up their pastoral pursuits.

There is a category of *Fulfulde*-speaking cattle pastoralists whom the *Fulɓe na'i* regard as 'different' (*feere*) from themselves and whom they call *Bororo'en*.

The term *Bororo'en* does not refer to a specific 'clan' or 'tribe' but to a general category of pastoralists who, although they are

[1] 'Fulani' is the Hausa name for the ethnic group. Hausa may also refer to Fulani as *Filani* and *Hilani*. Other names by which they are known are: *Fula* by Mandingo; *Fulata* by Kanuri; and *Peul* by the French.

'remote kin' (*min kowdi to wodɗi*, lit. 'we are related far off'), practise a different ecology, have different values, customs, and so forth.
Bororo'en in fact need hardly be mentioned in a study of the
pastoralists of Gwandu Emirate because in the area they are
numerically negligible. They favour large tracts of bush for
pasture such as are found today only in parts of French West
Africa, Bornu, and elsewhere, but not in Gwandu. *Fulɓe na'i* think
of the *Bororo'en* as having vast herds of cattle, being less tied to a
particular area, and knowing much about cattle medicines. But,
as Moslems, they add piously, the *Bororo'en* are practically infidels
—'their culture is inferior to ours' (*al'ada maɓɓe ɗum fotai al'ada
amin'*). While this comment is made in a disparaging way, *Fulɓe na'i*
think of the *Bororo'en* in other contexts in friendly terms, for they
say, 'do they not have cattle?'

Thus the society of the 'Fulani', using the term in its broadest
sense, includes a series of distinct sub-cultures. The way in which
the members of any sub-culture (*Torooɓe, Fulɓe siire, Fulɓe n'ai,*
and *Bororo'en*) see themselves in relation to any other sub-culture
is, of course, dependent upon the social or political context. It is
with the *Fulɓe na'i* that this study is concerned, for intensive study
was confined to them. Time did not permit a detailed study of the
other sub-cultures, nor was it included in the terms of reference of
the research project.

The 'Fulani', again using the term in its broadest sense, together
constitute a minority in the wider Hausa-speaking society of
which they are a part. Moreover, as will be seen below (see Census
Analysis) the *Fulɓe na'i* are a minority within that minority.

The majority of the population are negroid Hausa-speaking
people whom the *Fulɓe na'i* loosely call *Haaɓe* (s. *Kaaɗo*). In its
broadest usage the term *Haaɓe* may be used to refer to all negroid
peoples with whom they have contact or of whom they have
knowledge. The term may also be used in referring to *Torooɓe* and
to *Fulɓe siire* in a disparaging way by which they imply that
Torooɓe and *Fulɓe siire* have 'become *Haaɓe*' (*latike Haaɓe*); that is,
by intermarrying with *Haaɓe* and thus losing their 'racial purity'
and their cultural identity. In the same contexts as above, but
usually implying even greater disparagement, the *Fulɓe na'i* use the
term *baleeɓe* (s. *baleejo*, lit. 'black people'). In its narrowest sense
the word *Haaɓe* means the sedentary indigenous negroid inhabitants. If they wish to be more specific they speak of the

Hausanko'en, Kabanko'en, Yorubanko'en (negroid peoples of Hausa, Kebbi, and Yorubaland, respectively), and so forth.

Now the *Fulɓe na'i* consider themselves to be a homogeneous and distinctive group in relation to the *Torooɓe, Fulɓe siire, Bororo'en,* and *Haaɓe.* Provisionally (and here we must anticipate later data), we might link this to the fact that they move within a common territory, they are all more or less poor in cattle and depend on farming to supplement their resources, and to a relatively equal degree they share the faith in Islam. They possess in common a distinctive series of interests, problems, and values and it is because of these that they have a sense of solidarity.

Census Analysis

Sokoto Province has an area of 36,477 square miles and, according to the 1952 census, had a gross population of 2,679,841—a density of 73·4 per square mile. However, the population is by no means evenly distributed over the Province; 20 per cent. of the area is occupied by forest reserves in which residence is now prohibited; there are other large tracts of bush which are but thinly populated, or without residents, and as we shall see, a large percentage of the population is concentrated along the river valleys.

The following are the gross figures and densities for each of the four Emirates in the Province.

Emirate	Population	Area (sq. miles)	Density (per sq. mile)
Sokoto	2,020,340	25,608	78·8
Gwandu	416,579	6,207	67·1
Argungu	170,603	3,356	50·8
Yauri	72,319	1,306	66·3

While it is important to show the proportion, in the total population of the four Emirates, which is classified in the census as 'Fulani', only a fraction of those so listed are, in fact, pastoral peoples.[1] Thus the 'Fulani' population figures of the census include the following peoples:

1. The aristocratic *Torooɓe.*
2. The *Fulɓe siire* (settled agricultural).
3. The *Fulɓe na'i* (including a few *Bororo'en*).

[1] A 'pastoralist' may be defined, in the economic sense, as an individual who can and does lay claim to the resources of a herd for all or the greater part of his subsistence.

4. Miscellaneous:
  (*a*) *Fulfulde*-speaking ex-slaves and their descendants who
  may claim to be *Fulɓe* but are not recognized by the latter
  as such. A relatively small group in 'bush' areas.
  (*b*) A few *Haaɓe* who aspire to higher status by claiming to be
  Torooɓe.

The following are the figures, for each Emirate and for the
Province, of the gross Fulani population, their percentage of the
total population, and their density per square mile.

Emirate	Gross population	Non-Fulani population	Fulani	% Fulani	Density Fulani
Sokoto	2,020,340	1,703,368	316,972	15·6	12·3
Gwandu	416,579	358,690	57,889	12·7	9·3
Argungu	170,603	153,846	16,757	9·9	4·9
Yauri	72,319	67,636	4,683	6·4	3·5
Province	2,679,841	2,283,540	396,301	14·3	10·8

For arriving at reliable figures for the pastoral section of the
population the census was taken at an unfortunate time. During
July, when the figures were collected, many *Fulɓe* are moving from
the dry- to the wet-season camps. In consequence their location
could not be well known by the census takers. Moreover, in July
some members of households work on their farms while other
members of the same households tend their cattle many miles
away. This dispersal of the members of households provided herd-
owners with opportunities for not reporting some of their members;
an opportunity which they would welcome since they regard anything in the nature of a census as being related to a projected
increase in their tax. For these reasons the figures cited below are
likely to be in error on the conservative side. They are taken from
a report[1] based on more detailed unpublished returns than the
official census.

Emirate	Pastoral population	Area	Density
Sokoto	36,894	25,608	1·4
Gwandu	21,819	6,207	3·5
Argungu	9,569	3,356	2·8
Yauri	4,000	1,306	3·0
Province	72,282	36,477	1·9

[1] C. Hanson-Smith, Note on the Sokoto Fulɓe (unpublished manuscript), 1955.

Using the data of the previous tables we calculate: (1) the percentage of *Fulɓe na'i* to gross population; (2) the percentage of *Fulɓe na'i* to other 'Fulani'.

Emirate	Gross population	Gross Fulani population	Fulɓe na'i	% Gross population	% Gross Fulani
Sokoto .	2,020,340	316,972	36,894	1·8	11·6
Gwandu .	416,579	57,889	21,819	5·2	37·6
Argungu .	170,603	16,757	9,569	5·6	57·4
Yauri . .	72,319	4,683	4,000	5·5	86·2
Province .	2,679,841	396,301	72,282	2·6	18·2

The high percentage of non-pastoral Fulani in Sokoto and Gwandu Emirates reflects the fact that these areas are the traditional strongholds of the *Torooɓe*—'this is the land of the faithful'. But the statistics have also been affected by the consequences of the great rinderpest epidemic of 1887–91.[1] Prior to this there were many *Fulɓe na'i* in what is now Sokoto Emirate—and to a lesser extent in Gwandu Emirate. With the loss of their herds many of these pastoralists were obliged to turn to farming. In Argungu and Yauri Emirates the relatively low gross Fulani population reflects the feelings of both the *Fulɓe siire* and *Fulɓe na'i* that these are 'unpleasant' (*wela*) Emirates in which to live. *Fulɓe* of this region feel that Gwandu and Sokoto Emirates are their 'home'. Nevertheless, owing to land pressure elsewhere, there has been a considerable pastoral influx into Yauri and Argungu in the past forty or fifty years.

The inferences which we can draw from the above statistics are limited, so far as the pastoral density is concerned, for the simple reason that because of their movement local densities vary seasonally and the figures are based on a count taken during only one month of the year. If the count were made late in the wet season or early in the dry season it is likely that Sokoto Emirate (much of which area is in the north of the Province) would show a higher density of *Fulɓe na'i*.

[1] See F. W. de St. Croix, *The Fulani of Northern Nigeria*, Lagos, 1944.

2

HISTORY AND TRADITIONS OF ORIGIN OF FULANI IN NORTHERN NIGERIA

THE origin of the Fulani has long been a matter of curiosity and conjecture among scholars. However, it is generally accepted that the forebears of all Fulani now living in the Western Sudan came from the Futa Toro (Senegal Basin).

Linguistic evidence supports the view that historically Fulani movement was from west to east. This is so because, although the Fulani language is spoken by considerably more than 4 millions[1] from Senegal to at least Wadai east of Lake Chad, only in the Senegal area are genetic relationships traced with local languages. In his linguistic analysis Greenberg shows a close structural relationship between the Fulani and the Serer-Sin and Wolof languages of the Senegal area and together they are classed as 'the northern sub-group of Westermann's West Atlantic Section of his West Sudan Family'.[2] It may be inferred that Senegal was an early nucleus from which Fulani spread eastward.

The *Infaku'l Maisuri*[3] mentions the tradition that an Arab, Ukuba, married a woman of Futa Toro and from this marriage four sons were born, Duti, Nas, Wiya, and Arabu. Ukuba later returned to Arabia leaving his children with their mother. These children were the first Fulani and they spoke a language which had never been heard before—Fulfulde. Today it is very rarely that one meets Fulɓe na'i in Western Sokoto Province who have knowledge of any myth of origin. A few among them know one or more details or variations of the above myth; some of them for example

---

[1] Diedrich Westermann and M. A. Bryan, *Handbook of African Languages, Part II, The Languages of West Africa*, London, 1952; Jacques Richard-Molard in his *Afrique Occidentale Française*, Paris, 1949, p. 95, estimates that there are 4½ million Fulani speakers.

[2] Joseph H. Greenberg, 'Studies in African Linguistic Classification: The Classification of Fulani', *South-western Journal of Anthropology*, vol. v. 2, 1949, pp. 190-8.

[3] Written by Bello, son of Usman Dan Fodio, translated by E. J. Arnett in *The Rise of the Sokoto Fulani*.

may know only Ukuba's name and perhaps that he was an Arab, others may not know his name, but they 'heard' he came from the east (or that he was an Arab); in other cases the name of Ukuba's wife (Bajjomangu, or Bajjomanga) may be recalled. Whatever the variations of the myth Ukuba and his wife are credited with having sons only. Informants are rarely specific as to the number of sons; some said they did not know while others mentioned two or four, one informant said there were twelve. The names of the sons are rarely remembered; significantly, however, one informant mentioned that the 'senior son's name was Muusa and in him the Torooɓe originated' (. . . *Muusa ko woni maudo maɓɓe Muusa i kanko non Torooɓe 'yiwi*). Since primogeniture is important it is congruent that the aristocrats (*mauɓe*) are thought to have descended from a senior son.

It is not possible to establish the precise date at which the eastward migration of Torooɓe and Fulɓe na'i began. However, it is known that they were in Hausaland as early as the thirteenth century and that the first penetration was gradual and peaceful.[1]

Unfortunately most of the written chronicles which existed in the Hausa states were destroyed in the *Jihad*, but it is generally believed that Islam reached Kano in the fourteenth century and was brought by the Wangarawa or Mandingo from Mali. Katsina appears to have become Islamized about the same time, for to this period is ascribed the first *sarkin* (H. chief, leader, commander, or king) to have a Moslem name, Muhammad.

Later in the fourteenth century Kano and Katsina lapsed into paganism, but they experienced a revival late in the fifteenth century under the influence of the famous apostle El Maghili of Tlemcen (Algeria). El Maghili travelled and preached at Air, Takedda, Katsina, and Kano where he was esteemed as a wise counsellor both in religious and political matters. He reached Gao in 1502 where he had much influence over Askia the Great, king of the Songhai Empire.

The early Islamic stimulus received by the Hausa-speaking peoples was not sufficient to prevent another gradual lapse into paganism after the departure of El Maghili. And there was no significant revival until the Fulani Jihad.

[1] E. W. Bovill, *Caravans of the Old Sahara*, London, 1933, pp. 223-4. This is an extremely good book on the long and exciting history of the Western Sudan. It gives a background for the study of any community in the region.

At the beginning of the sixteenth century the Hausa states were flanked by the powerful kingdoms of Songhai to the west and Bornu to the east. In 1513 Askia the Great of Songhai accompanied by Kanta, who later founded the Kebbi Dynasty (1516),[1] waged a campaign in which most of the Hausa states were defeated—Zamfara and Kano were captured and the rulers of Gobir, Katsina, and Zaria were killed. Songhai did not, however, maintain its domination for long and by the end of the sixteenth century Katsina had become a vassal of Bornu and continued as such for 200 years.

During the eighteenth century Katsina flourished as an important centre in the desert trade but later gave way to Kano. In the middle of the century the Gobirawa moved south from Asben into Zamfara and here they came into conflict with Katsina. These are but a few of the main events leading to the close of the eighteenth century. By the end of the century Bornu was the undisputed power of the north-east, dominating Kano and probably Katsina and Zaria as well. The non-Hausa chiefdom of Nupe was independent, but not very powerful, in the south. Gobir had risen to a position of considerable power in the north-west and Kebbi, having revolted against Songhai in 1516, still maintained its independence in the west.

While these events were taking place the influx of Torooɓe (and perhaps other non-pastoral 'clans') and Fulɓe na'i continued, and they had reached significant numbers by the beginning of the nineteenth century.

Now in 1754 Usuman (Usumanu) the son of Fodio, a Toroodo, was born at Marata near Birnin Konni (a few miles north of the present Sokoto provincial boundary in the French Niger Province) in Gobirland. Usuman was keenly interested in religion and he, together with his brother Abdullahi (later the first Emir of Gwandu), was instructed in the Koran by Jibrilla and in Maliki Law by Rissala and other authorities.

Fulɓe na'i[2] today, in describing Usuman, speak of him as having been inspired by God, being extremely learned, having a likeable personality, and having been a persuasive preacher. From the accounts of the informants as well as from literature there seems little doubt that he was uncommonly sincere and was convinced

---

[1] Among the Zabermawa and Arewa peoples.
[2] From this point forward when referring to the Fulɓe na'i the shorter term Fulɓe (s. Pullo) will be used.

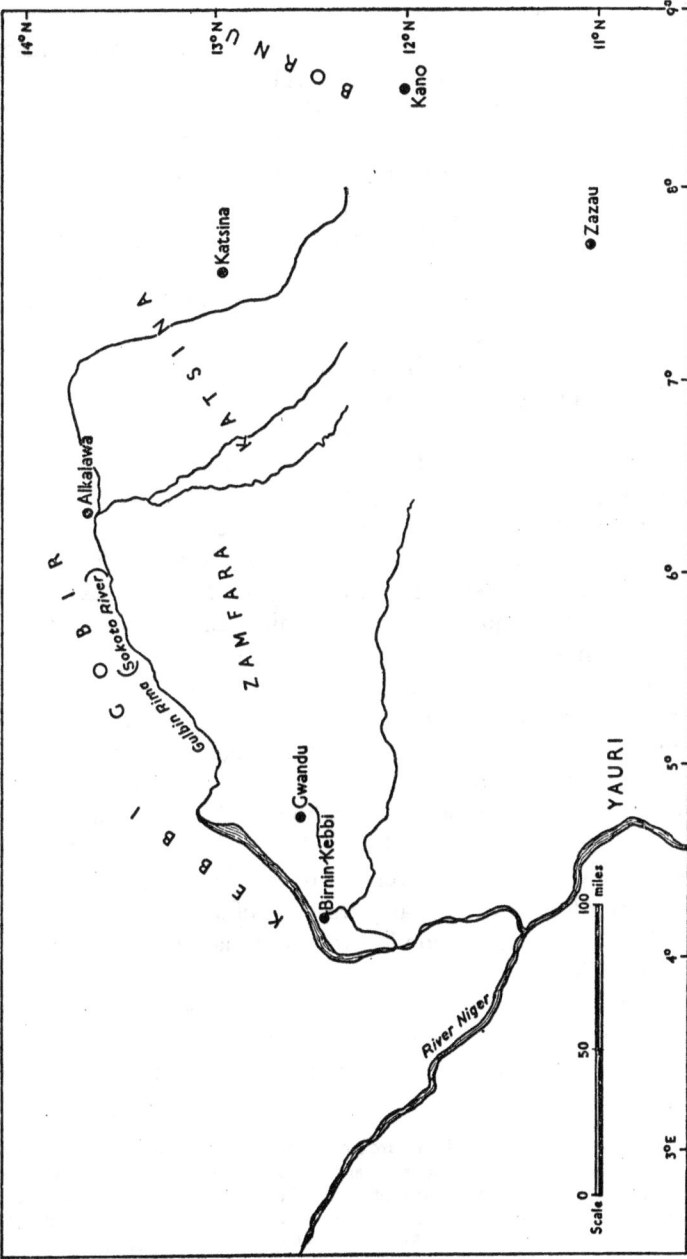

Fig. 1. Pre-Jihad rival kingdoms.

of his personal mission—to devote his life to the purification of the debased form of Mohammedanism in the Western Sudan.

It seems unlikely that Usuman would have gained a following from among the Fulɓe to wage his Jihad[1] (F. *Jihadi*) were it not for the fact that pastoralists found conditions in Gobir intolerable. The most enthusiastic support came in the beginning from those Fulɓe who knew him personally in the early days of his preaching and saw in him a means of overcoming the oppression of Sarkin Gobir. Sarkin Gobir Bawa Jan Gwarzo (1776–94) is still remembered for the hearty contempt in which he held the Fulɓe. Bawa had attempted to collect tribute from the herdsmen by giving titles (*Ausa, Dabrun,* and *Saara*) to selected Fulɓe from among his following in the hope that they would gather revenue for him. When this failed, Fulɓe say, he turned to frequent raiding of the camps of the *Konningko'en* (near the town of Birnin Konni in the French Niger Province)—and perhaps others for which there is no information—and carried the booty off to the Gobir capital at Alkalawa.[2] As at this time the Fulɓe were not able to offer effective resistance some of them fled, it is said, to Bornu. Others were loath to make a long journey to an unfamiliar country which, for all they knew, might not offer better conditions. Konningko'en informants affirm that at that time Kebbi would have been no improvement on Gobir as a place to live.

Bawa was succeeded by his younger brothers Yakuba (1794–1800) and Nafata (1800–2). It was the latter who made the infamous declaration that only those who were born Mohammedans could practise the religion, and he forbade men to wear robes and turbans and women to wear veils. Modern Fulɓe add that he also forbade their forefathers to carry weapons of any kind—an indication of the mounting tension between Usuman and his following and Sarkin Gobir.

It was not until after Yunfa, son of Nafata and former pupil of Usuman, became Sarkin Gobir (1802) that the Jihad began. Yunfa regarded the growing influence of Usuman as a threat to his own power and it was only a matter of time until an open breach de-

---

[1] The salient events of the Jihad are not detailed here as they are well documented elsewhere. For the present we are merely concerned with noting a few points which are of interest because of their relation to data which follow. For further information on the Jihad and subsequent political developments see S. J. Hogben, *The Mohammedan Emirates of Nigeria*, London, 1930.

[2] On the *Gulbin Rima* (Sokoto River) north-east of Sokoto city.

veloped between them. One of the first incidents occurred when Usuman had the chains removed from some believers who were being taken prisoner on Yunfa's orders. This event so enraged Yunfa that he plotted the death of Usuman who was saved—so it was believed—by divine power. His escape from the attempt on his life made Usuman an even more popular figure and further alarmed Yunfa. With increased determination to kill Usuman, Yunfa set out to attack the former at his town at Degel. This was the occasion of Usuman's famous flight (*hijra*, 21 February 1804) to Gudu where the Moslems, conscious of their strength, were further inspired by the zeal of the preacher.

The first battle occurred near Tabkin (lake) Kwotto as the faithful defended themselves against Yunfa on 21 June. The hardy mounted warriors of Gobir were defeated by the skilled pastoral bowmen and Haaɓe converts. Moslem victors captured horses which they had previously been forbidden to own and which greatly increased their military potential. Victory was interpreted as divine approval of the believers' actions and they solemnly declared a holy war on the infidels. Usuman was chosen as their leader with the title 'King of the Faithful' (*Lamiiɗo Julɓe*, H. *Sarkin Musulmi*).

After his defeat Yunfa sent a warning to the Hausa sister states advising them of the danger of the new movement, for he correctly appraised the ambitions of his rebels.

News of the initial success of Shehu (or Shefu, as Usuman was now called) against Gobir—a powerful kingdom with long experience in warfare against the rugged and skilful Tuareg—travelled quickly through the open country of the Sudan, and it was not without an aura of divine blessing surrounding Shehu and his devotees. The oppressed looked to Shehu for deliverance; the ambitious joined him in the hope of gaining power. Thus, repeating a pattern familiar in the long history of war in the Western Sudan, the weak sought the support and protection of the strong. The trusted followers of Shehu received flags from him and with Shehu's blessings went into battle. In rapid succession many Hausa states were conquered as Fulani rule penetrated to the western reaches of Bornu.

Despite their early success in battle against Gobir the Moslem forces did not finally conquer them until 1808 when Bello, the son of Shehu, in a well-planned campaign captured Alkalawa and killed Yunfa. After this event Gobir did not recover her former strength.

Early in the Jihad Shehu realized that so long as Kebbi maintained her strength and independence she would be a threat to him. Accordingly, in 1805 he sent Abdullahi, his younger brother, to attack the capital at Birnin Kebbi. Sarkin Kebbi (Muhammadu Fodi dan Salema) fled from the town and, although neither he nor his successors recaptured Birnin Kebbi, they maintained an active resistance from Argungu until the British occupation. In order to decentralize the administration of the Empire and perhaps also in recognition of the strength of Kebbi, Shehu decided to partition the conquered territory. Thus in 1809 he placed his younger brother Abdullahi in charge of the western kingdom—Nupe Yauri, Illo, Gurma, and Borgu—and his son Bello in charge of the eastern kingdom—the Hausa states, Adamawa, and parts of Bornu. To his old friend Alieu Jedo (of the pastoral Konningko'en clan) in recognition of his heroic fighting in the early days of the Jihad, Shehu gave the title of *Sarkin Yaki* (H., war leader) and placed him in charge of the north, although Alieu was to be subordinate to Bello. With capitals at Sokoto (eastern region) and Gwandu (western region) it might be argued that it would be easier to defend the Fulani Empire against skirmishes with Kebbi. Until his death in 1817 Shehu remained as a sort of commander in chief, although from 1809, when Bello built Sokoto for his father, the latter devoted himself to study, leaving practical administration in the hands of Bello and Abdullahi. In 1817 Bello fulfilled the death wish of his father by accepting the title 'King of the Faithful' and thus became the Moslem leader for the whole of the Fulani Kingdom and the administrative head for the eastern region. At the beginning of Bello's reign Abdullahi was incensed at not gaining the office for, in virtue of the spiritual leadership of Sokoto, the office of Sarkin Gwandu (now held by Abdullahi) was inferior. However, throughout the history of the Empire the relations between the two courts have always been most congenial and they are described by the natives as elder and younger brothers.

The literature is notably unhelpful with regard to information concerning the pastoralists both before and after the Jihad. Regrettably, for reasons which are apparent below, knowledge of the pastoralists today can only in a generalized way fill this important gap. Indeed, from the point of view of studying the foundations of the Empire and details of its subsequent administration, the pastoralists are not the proper subjects of study. This information is best collected from informants in the capitals of Sokoto, Gwandu, and other centres and, for practical reasons, it had, more or less, to be excluded from the present research. The reason for this obscurity is that whereas, as we have seen, some (but not all) pastoralists saw the possibility of advantage in joining (and did join) the Moslem forces, the fact remains that to a very large extent the pastoralists did not become more than peripherally attached to the actual administration of the Empire. The key positions in the administration were, as noted above, held by Tooroɓe not only in virtue of their learning in Islam but also because, being sedentary people living among the Haaɓe, they understood the latter and some of them had pre-Jihad administrative experience in the Haaɓe states. In contrast the herdsmen as a group were without learning at the time the Jihad began and their interests were largely confined to good husbandry of their cattle. Thus between the Tooroɓe and the pastoralists there was a cultural dichotomy which had its origin perhaps several centuries before the Jihad and which has persisted to the present day.

Most pastoral informants cannot give a single detail of their ancestors' social and political life in pre-Jihad times. But the information obtained shows that the herdsmen lived in rather large and mobile bush encampments in which they were prepared either to defend themselves or to flee, depending upon the strength of their enemies. Their contacts with and their economic dependence on the Haaɓe was much less than it was after the Jihad and is today. Their diet was largely of milk (not of corn as today) and they were clothed in hides and skins instead of robes and turbans from the markets. Undoubtedly there were trade relations with the Haaɓe but on a smaller scale than after the Jihad and in modern times.

The Jihad brought about a change in the life of the pastoralists which was no less important than the change which came 100 years later with the British conquest. Prior to the Jihad the pastoralists, as subject peoples, were not allowed to own slaves, but with victory in the Holy War their status changed from subject peoples to part of an *élite*. Moreover, from the booty of war and from tribute from the vassal states paid to Sokoto and Gwandu, slaves were available in great numbers. But if slaves were available they

were also in considerable demand for building walled villages
because much of the territory which now lies in western Sokoto
and Gwandu Emirates was subject to frequent raids from Kebbi
which continued until the British occupation.

Some indication of the insecurity within the Empire is given in
the journal of the German explorer, Dr. Henry Barth, who was in
Gwandu in May 1853.

> . . . the insecurity of the neighbourhood was so great that it was not
> possible, at least in a northerly direction, to proceed many yards from
> the wall. Several times during my stay [19 days] the alarm was given
> that the enemy was approaching and the whole political state of the
> place was plunged into the most terrible disorder, the enemy [Kebbi]
> being established in several strong places at scarcely half a days journey
> distance . . . a numerous foray left early in the morning of 29th May, but
> returned the same evening. . . . They had, however, only given an addi-
> tional proof of their cowardly disposition, inasmuch as they had not even
> dared to attack the enemy. . . .[1]

It is important to stress the regular aggression of Kebbi (and to
a lesser extent Gobir, Illo, and Bussa) during the nineteenth
century for, as we have seen, while the Empire embraced a wide
territory there was little security of life and property until the
British conquest. The above citation shows how Kebbi threatened
the very capital at Gwandu, and indeed, during the fifty years
between the visit of Barth to Gwandu and the British victory
Kebbi appears to have grown stronger in her struggle against the
Fulani Empire. But before noting later developments we must
first outline certain of the social and political fortunes of the
pastoralists shortly after the Jihad.

After the Moslem forces had demonstrated a degree of success,
Haaɓe living in a bush village would make submission to a local
pastoral clan or sub-clan leader (variously called *'ardo, dikko,
jonwuro,* and *rugga*), promise their allegiance and, in return, seek
protection.[2] The pastoral leader in turn would go to the local
capital at Gwandu or Sokoto and, after pledging his allegiance,
would receive a title, usually *Sarkin* or *Lamiiɗo,* and a gown and
turban as a symbol of state recognition. A claimant to such office
had to have an adequate number of clients before a title would be

---

[1] H. Barth, *Barth's Travels in Africa*, London, 1890, vol. ii, p. 194.

[2] Informants describe events only in the broadest outline. It is not possible
today to get much detail of past events nor to be sure of their chronology.

granted to him. In order to acquire the requisite number he might claim the allegiance of a series of contiguous hamlets or small villages. Others could gain a title by being locally acknowledged as the head of a single village if it were of sufficient size. Generally speaking, in what is now Gwandu Emirate, any village with a sufficient labour force to build its own wall could be directly represented at the capital. Such villages might give protection to and claim the allegiance of smaller villages and hamlets nearby. But the pattern by which the local village and district community was linked with their respective capital is far too complicated to be detailed in a brief historical sketch, even if our data were complete. However, it should be noted that the success of the Jihad did attract a good many pastoral emigrants to the area surrounding Sokoto and to a lesser extent Gwandu. Pastoralists came with their slaves 'to be near Shehu'—in some cases they lived in open villages and paid allegiance directly to Sokoto. In other cases they lived within fiefs which had been awarded to distinguished supporters of the Jihad, and to them they paid the annual tithes (*gaisuwa*).

While for such a large area as Sokoto and Gwandu Emirates it is dangerous to make broad generalizations, it is important to mention that the Jihad, bringing as it did much instability, compelled the herdsmen to live in or near walled villages where they became local *élites*. So far as one can tell they welcomed the opportunity of enjoying the greater comfort of sedentary living and having slaves to lighten the burden of gaining a livelihood. The ownership of cattle continued to be an important item in prestige ranking and the maintenance of pastoral values persisted. But, added to the traditional status attached to cattle-ownership, was competition for the possession of slaves and a reputation for learning in Islam. With their slaves occupied both in farming and in tending cattle, some herd-owners and their children used their leisure time to study.

Not all pastoralists were equally affected by the emergence of the Torooɓe as aristocrats and the revival of interest in Islam. In remote areas of minor strategic value there was little interference with the *status quo*—at least so far as changing traditional values was concerned. Both Gwandu and Sokoto were too much concerned with recurrent crises with Kebbi and Gobir to restrict the autonomy of such herdsmen.

For much of the interval between the beginning of the Jihad and the British conquest (99 years) there seems to have been no area in what is now western Sokoto Province which could entirely relax its defences. For even if there were a lull in the general turmoil, it was felt that eventually a crisis would occur. From the pastoral point of view one of their greatest crises—the outbreak of rinderpest epidemic—probably did arise directly from the widespread insecurity and consequent restriction of movement of their cattle. For many years cattle were emaciated owing to confinement within the walls and precincts of villages and finally, according to modern accounts, the majority of the bovine population died in the great rinderpest epidemic of 1887–91.[1] Some herd-owners lost all their beasts while others were left with only one or two animals with which to begin another herd. Some were able to barter their slaves in order to obtain a cow or a calf.

Eleven years after the epidemic (*sannu*) the British forces took Gwandu and Argungu (Kebbi) without a fight and the next year, having failed to negotiate peaceful relations, they attacked and captured Sokoto in less than a day's fighting. The battle took place on 19 March 1903 and by the end of the month Sir Fredrick Lugard was to quote Major Burdon, Resident at Sokoto, as follows:

... everything is settling down peacefully ... the Sultan and chiefs gave willing assistance in every way ... the original Hausa rulers are very pleased with us for having avenged their defeat on the Fulani, but they show no signs of wanting to assert their independence.[2]

Gwandu in particular was pleased to be relieved of the almost continuous raiding from Kebbi. The pastoralists, having not yet recovered from the loss of their herds in the rinderpest epidemic, welcomed the security brought by the Protectorate and were soon to take advantage of their opportunity for dispersal in search of better grazing; but they did find it distressing to be dispossessed of their slaves while the strength of their herds was only beginning to recover from an unprecedented low level.

In a later section we shall discuss in more detail some features of pastoral social and political life during the period of the Fulani Empire and also the social changes following the establishment of the Protectorate.

[1] de St. Croix, op. cit., p. 5.
[2] *Colonial Reports*, Northern Nigeria, 1903, p. 174.

3

THE ENVIRONMENTAL SETTING

SOKOTO Province lies entirely within the Sudanese savannah zone, that vast expanse of open country lying between 8° and 16° N. In its general features the Province is typical of the zone of which it is a part. And since, in any region which supports human inhabitants, the climate and physical environment are basic considerations in the study of a society, it is necessary to describe, in a general way, the environmental features.

The usual scenery is an almost monotonous extension of undulating plains with an average elevation of 1,000 feet above sea-level. Some scenic variety is found, however, in the irregular occurrence of conical and flat-topped hills which normally reach a height of several hundred feet above the surrounding country-side.[1] Very often water erosion has removed most of the topsoil so that the hills are not suitable for horticulture although they may support a sparse cover of trees and grass. In many areas accidental and deliberate bush burning contributes to an increase in the already high rate of erosion occasioned by torrential rains falling on irregular terrain. Of course, as in other parts of Northern Nigeria erosion is most serious where the land gradient is steep, but it may also occur even where the land is quite level, especially when there is regular grass burning which prevents effective humus formation.

There is a noticeable reduction in the height and density of vegetation as one moves from south to north which is directly correlated with the decrease of rainfall in the higher latitudes. But despite these differences in the northern and southern extremities the area may be loosely described as orchard bush. In certain districts farming is now practised so intensively that the country-side, being either under active cultivation or in a state of recovery, does not appear in its virgin condition. Surrounding towns, villages, and hamlets are tracts of open country—farm clearings—the extent of which is dependent upon the size of the compact settlement. The farmed area is generally dotted with trees which

[1] For the geological details see Brynmor Jones, *The Sedimentary Rocks of Sokoto Province*, Geological Survey of Nigeria, Bulletin No. 18, Government Printers, Lagos, 1948.

may have economic value or, owing to the difficulty of clearing, were left by the farm-owner and act as shade trees during the rest periods taken by the farmers when they are working on the land.

As in other parts of the Western Sudan there are two marked seasons—the wet and the dry. Practically all the rain falls between the months of June and September and for about a month in the middle of this period rain falls almost every day.

Monthly rainfall figures are given below for Sokoto city and Birnin Kebbi—averages over periods of 36 and 33 years respectively up to and including 1951.[1] It is unfortunate that data showing the year-to-year variations are not available—for these are very considerable and important in an area in which, on an average, the rainfall is barely adequate.

Sokoto (13° 3′ N., 5° 14′ E.)

Jan.	Feb.	Mar.	Apr.	May	June	July	Aug.	Sept.	Oct.	Nov.	Dec.
0·0	0·0	0·0	0·4	2·0	3·5	5·8	9·3	5·7	0·5	0·0	0·0

Average total annual rainfall Sokoto town: 27·2 inches.

Birnin Kebbi (12° 28′ N., 4° 11′ E.)

Jan.	Feb.	Mar.	Apr.	May	June	July	Aug.	Sept.	Oct.	Nov.	Dec.
0·0	0·0	0·2	0·5	2·5	4·3	6·9	10·8	5·7	0·7	0·0	0·0

Average total annual rainfall Birnin Kebbi: 31·6 inches.

Although the latitude difference between Sokoto and Birnin Kebbi is just over one half of a degree (35 miles) it is seen that Sokoto has, on an annual average, 4·4 inches less rainfall than does Birnin Kebbi. This shows how sharply average rainfall decreases with increase in latitude in this climatic zone—Sokoto being the more northerly has the lower rainfall. So far as one can tell this rainfall gradient is linked exclusively with difference in latitude between the two sites. There is no other factor, such as mountains or large bodies of water, which might produce local climatic effects. The ecological significance of comparatively heavy rainfall to the south and relatively light rainfall to the north must be stressed. The pattern of transhumance is described below, but it is appropriate to mention in this context that it is rainfall, its amount and distribution, which basically regulates the seasonal movements of pastoralists. Generally speaking, where rainfall is heavy pastoral conditions are unkind during the wet season, but by the same token the grasslands do not deteriorate as quickly in the dry season as do

[1] *The Nigeria Handbook*, 1953.

pastures where rain is light. Conversely, where there is little rain-fall the natural conditions for herdsmen are at their best in the wet season. For these reasons the main stream of cattle movement is northward for the wet season and southward for the dry season.

The first sign of the approach of the wet season appears in March when one can notice a gradual increase in relative humidity.[1] This is associated with a change in wind from the dry north-easterly system (Harmattan) to the comparatively moist south-westerly wind system. With the arrival of humid south-westerly air mass cloud formations begin to appear—first the high cirrus cloud during the day followed by clouds of vertical development (*cumulo nimbus*) in the evening. Associated with the latter are gale force winds and electric storms. The rainy season begins with in-frequent line squall showers which occur at night and, as the rainy season progresses, these increase in frequency. Finally, after the Harmattan air system has been displaced by the south-westerly system and the ground is moist from many showers, low stratus clouds appear, and rain may fall at any period in the day. The re-verse of this general pattern is repeated, although somewhat more abruptly, as the wet season ends in October.

The uneven nature, both in time and in space, of the early rain-fall in the wet season is an important factor in the growing process, particularly of early maturing species of corn and of grass. *Gero* (bulrush millet, *pennisetum typhoideum*), being the first crop planted, is said by farmers to be especially susceptible to the vagaries of the early wet season. It was observed that both the yield and the time required for maturation of *gero* was considerably affected (and varied locally) by the amount and distribution of early rains.

The climate is hot during the greater part of the year, but only for a period of about six weeks immediately before and after the rains do the inhabitants complain seriously of excessive heat. During these hot seasons shade temperatures may go to a maxi-mum of about 110° F., but discomfort is felt because of the high relative humidity which inhibits body cooling. In the wet season the temperatures still remain relatively high, but because the 'ground is cool' (i.e. damp) and also because cloud cover is frequent,

[1] The relative humidity figures for Kano (12° N., 8° 31′ E.) the only ones available, are probably lower than those for Gwandu Emirate in both the dry and the wet seasons. The average figures for Kano are 90 per cent. at dawn and 60 per cent. in the afternoon in the wet season; and in the dry season 35 per cent. at dawn and 12 per cent. in the afternoon.

they do not complain even though the relative humidity is high. Indeed, considering the whole year, discomfort through cold is greater than that due to heat. Pastoralists feel uncomfortably cold at night during the wet season and also during the Harmattan—from about December until March. This is because of a poorly balanced diet and inadequate or no shelters. In the Harmattan the diurnal variation reaches its maximum which may be up to 50°. While people of all ages complain of the cold it is felt most seriously by the very young and the aged—especially during the hour or two before dawn. Those who can, sleep in a shelter and, if possible, near a fire. That the inhabitants really feel the cold is seen in the fact that it was rarely possible to convince them that lands do exist which have a colder climate than theirs.

It is important to mention the drainage system of the region, for the two principal rivers, the Sokoto and the Niger, stand at the very base of the cattle economy because without them the area would be able to support only a fraction of the cattle population which it does at present. The great value of the rivers is not confined to the pastoralists alone. The sedentary inhabitants have considerable skill and elaborate techniques in fishing, and large quantities of fish, both fresh and dried, find their way to markets which are often a considerable distance from the rivers. It is clear that fish provide a valuable source of protein over a comparatively wide area.

The Niger enters the Province at the French border near Illo. In Gwandu Emirate it is a broad stream which flows through a flood-plain several miles in width upon which succulent grasses flourish. The channel of the river is flanked by numerous sand-banks which provide clean resting places for cattle not at pasture. The channel is also interspersed with many fertile grassy islands which were important in the past for they acted as easily defended camp-sites when the herdsmen were attacked by their enemies. Today they are important not only as pastures but also as places of retreat in the growing season when there is risk of damage to the crops of sedentary peoples.

The confluence of the Sokoto and Niger Rivers is near Bahindi. While the Sokoto River carries a far smaller volume of water than the Niger it is of great importance for it too has a broad flood-plain (varying in width from one or two miles to a maximum of eight miles) which provides indispensable pastures in the dry

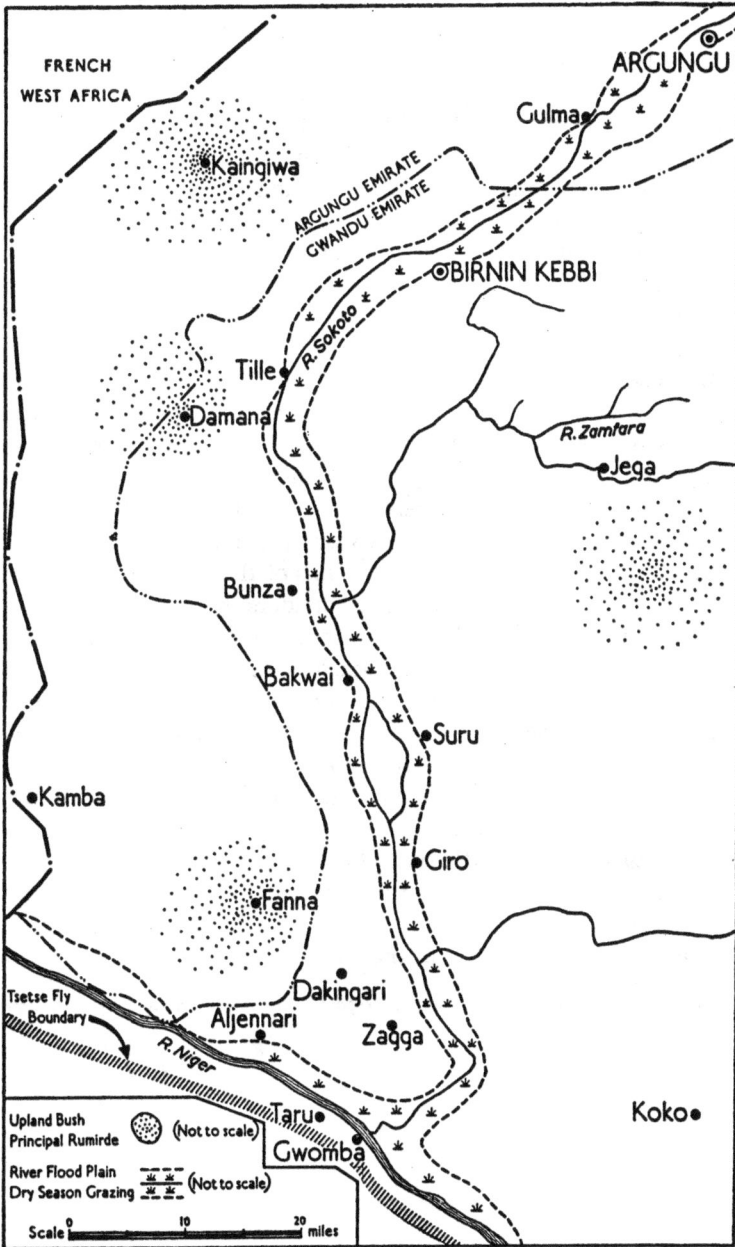

FIG. 2. Area of field study: the riverain and upland bush area.

season when upland pastures have been parched by the sun and burned by bush fires. The Sokoto River, unlike the Niger, is of great importance to the peasant farmers also for it is very suitable for dry-season farming. In addition, the fact that swamp-land is rejuvenated annually by deposits of alluvium gives it special value since yearly cropping is possible. Gwandu Fulɓe are fortunate in that, apart from a comparatively small section of the southern portion of the division,[1] the area is free from tsetse fly. Were it not for this fact, their system of transhumance would be more complicated and, one might venture to suggest, the region would be less favoured by graziers.

Because of their common interests in the flood-plain it is not surprising to find the greatest concentration of pastoralists and farmers within easy reach of the Sokoto River in particular. In comparison with flood-land, the upland bush is not restricted. However, the effect of farmers cultivating both flood-lands and uplands from a single home means that the most intensive upland cultivation is also found near the banks of the Sokoto River. The result of this is that there are long corridors of cultivated uplands flanking the flood-plain. Now it has been said that pastoral movements are southward in the dry season and northward in the wet season. But they must also move into the flood-plain in the dry season and into the upland bush in the wet season. Thus in order to meet their ecological needs herdsmen must have seasonally appropriate access to both the flood-land and the upland bush. But without enclosure and without an adequate number of well-demarcated and recognized cattle trails it is not possible, in these circumstances, to guarantee the protection of the interests of both pastoralists and farmers as they each, in their own way, go about gaining their livelihood from the land.

[1] See map, p. 21, and also map in *Report of the Nigerian Livestock Mission*, 1950.

4

FULƁE INTEREST IN THEIR CATTLE

IN writing of the Fulɓe it is necessary at the outset to consider the relation of cattle to their social system. A discussion of cattle at this stage, in the absence of ethnographic data, must necessarily be superficial and it should be regarded as merely an introduction to some basic concepts, to be elaborated in later sections, against which to view and interpret values and institutions within the society. A research worker among the Fulɓe can do much to enhance his status and gain rapport if, at an early stage, he shows a deep interest in cattle and some knowledge of their husbandry. Indeed, the herdsmen's confidence cannot be gained without this qualification.

Pastoralists value cattle far beyond either their utilitarian or their pecuniary worth. Among men, and to a slightly lesser extent among women, in the daily conversations in the camps and markets, cattle are discussed, directly or indirectly, more than any other topic. The needs of the herds basically determine the size and distribution of local groupings and, as we shall see, have an influence upon the nature of the relationships which obtain between the Fulɓe and the Haaɓe. On another plane it is important to stress that it is cattle ownership which binds the pastoralists together as a group within the plural society and with a degree of solidarity which transcends both kinship and clanship. To the owners and their direct dependants cattle are the symbol of membership within a group, the cohesion of whose proud members is maintained by a common body of interests and values.

The cattle-owning units are the simple and the compound family —these are the basic economic units. Since property in cattle normally passes in the male line women do not usually hold cattle to the same extent as men do. The conviction that 'men should own the cattle and women should own the milk' (*worɓe jei na'i reuɓe jei ɓiraaɗam*) is firmly held. Large-scale cattle-ownership by women is regarded as (and is in fact) anomalous. However successful a man may be as a husbandman he continues his endeavours to increase his stock.

For young boys in particular an interest in cattle and the desire to own them begin early; such interest pervades the enculturation process which begins in early childhood. Before children can walk they are brought into contact with calves of the camp for both may share the shade of a common tree or crude shelter during the long hours of sunshine. By the time a boy is about five years of age his fantasies, as indicated by his play, show a basic understanding of the significance of cattle in his society. He and his age fellows may build a miniature camp in which one of the most important details is a corral heavily populated with cattle. Significantly, fantasies expressing an interest in cattle, in the few cases observed, were seen to develop before, for example, a boy visualizes himself in the role of a husband. The building of such camps is an imitation of similar play observed among other older boys. The 'herds' in the model camps seen were small stones, but adult informants said that sometimes cattle are modelled in clay.

The play of young girls does not show the same interest in the corral, but it does show a remarkable interest in the formal layout of the camp. Girls play in larger groups than boys, see plate III, p. 112 (usually only two boys play together), and the age span may be greater—ages from about 6 to 12 years. Their model camps emphasize their interest in the care of milk products and the rearing of children. They make calabash platforms and stock them with miniature calabashes and other household utensils. Girls of 6 or 7 years of age who are deficient in women's lore are instructed by slightly older girls who are more knowledgeable.

The description of children's play shows how early in childhood adult roles are anticipated. There is a clear-cut dichotomy along sexual lines—the boys' interest in cattle and the girls' interest in the care of dairy products and the rearing of children.

Adult Fulɓe being themselves interested in cattle impart their enthusiasm to the children of the camp. Small boys gravitate towards the corral as they begin to develop 'intelligence' (*hakkilo*). At about the age of 5 they are given the task of keeping calves away from the domestic supply of grain and when they are about 6 years old they tie up the calves in the evening so that they will not feed from their dams. At this age also a boy will help to drive the cattle from the camp in the morning, but he will return when they have settled in their pastures under the care of an older attendant. The age of 7 is uniformly given as the age at which a boy is considered old enough to spend the entire day with the cattle, generally along with his father or elder brother, but in some cases he may herd alone. If he does not already know the elaborate cattle calls (*nodal na'i*) he will begin to learn them, will drive up stragglers, and act as assistant to the herdsman who is in charge. There is much lore of cattle-tending which he will begin to learn at this time; the types of grass which most appeal to cattle and the general dietary needs of the herd. The learning process is a combination of instruction at pasture and in the camps, what he overhears from those who have more experience, and prolonged observation and imitation. Through his questioning he will learn the genealogy of the herd and by observation he will come to know the 'character' (*gikku*) of each of the animals which is under his care. He will come to have favourite animals within the herd and for these he may pick succulent grasses and gather foliage from the trees.

As a boy grows older his responsibility is increased by his father according to the competence he shows. By the age of 9 a boy is usually capable of herding however unfavourable the conditions.

Herding calls for considerable skill and much agility; it is also extremely arduous. In the wet season, when grass is abundant, the cattle do not remain at pasture for more than five or six hours, leaving late in the morning and returning replete by 4 o'clock in the afternoon. But in this season there is the constant fear of their causing damage to Haaɓe crops and also getting drenched in the rain. Yet the dry season is the more difficult for, with sparse pastures, the cattle have long grazing hours; they leave at 7 o'clock in the morning and do not return for twelve hours. During the whole of this time a herd-boy takes no nourishment—he does not even drink milk as the cattle refuse to be milked when they are at pasture separated from their calves. Boys do not delude themselves that herding under these circumstances is a pleasant task, but they continue to feel that cattle are a priceless possession. With few exceptions they accept the view of adults that, since there are now no slaves, herding is the rightful task of the young who are healthy and energetic and hence can withstand the arduousness of the life ('they are in the midst of their youth, they have strength, they can withstand hardship', *ɓe chaka sukaaku, ɓe ngodi sembe ɓe mbowi torra*). Herd-boys comfort themselves with the thought that they will one day have children of their own who will take the responsibility of herding; meanwhile, they reason, they must tend the herd well in order that they may have status, security, and a leisurely life when they grow old. Thus, when a youth grows older and has devoted his active years to tending cattle, he begins to develop a proprietary interest in the herd of his father.

There is no question that one of the principal motivating factors in the desire of Fulɓe men to obtain cattle is their desire to become head of an independent household. A man and his wife (or wives), their unmarried daughters and their young married sons, constitute an economically self-sufficient unit whether or not they live in co-residence with other households. It is comparatively rare to find simple or compound families living in isolation except for short periods. But whatever the size of the residential unit, a man with a wife and family does have the option of moving off should he find local conditions unpleasant or if, for any other reason, he wishes to live elsewhere. To attempt to build up a herd if one is without a wife and family is regarded as a futile venture, for herdsmen say, 'a man who seeks wealth but does not have a family seeks for riches in vain' (*kul neddo mo wala fuh ɓiɓɓe rartua risku ommo rartua banza*).

In concluding this section it is important to stress a basic Fulɓe concept which is both explicit and implicit in their society: cattle and Fulɓe have been mutually dependent from the remote past, and it is the duty of Fulɓe to bear children and to increase their wealth in cattle so that this symbiotic relationship may be continued indefinitely. Thus, in an important sense, the pastoralists feel that they hold their cattle in trust for future generations and they will say that they are entitled to use the resources of the corral only in a frugal way, for by living lavishly they are jeopardizing the inheritance of unborn generations. The herdsmen regard the Fulɓe-cattle relationship as a diatomic unity in which the destruction of either part of the unity will inevitably lead to the destruction of the other—'if one harms the cattle one harms the Fulɓe' (*kul neddo no memi na'i ommo memi Fulɓe*). They also say: 'If the cattle die the Fulɓe will die' (*kul na'i baati Fulɓe no mai*), and—perhaps their strongest statement on the value of cattle— 'cattle surpass (in the widest sense) everything, they are even greater than one's father and mother' (*na'i i ɓuri koomi, i ɓuri inna i baba fuh*).

Now if Fulɓe regard the bearing of children as one of their most serious obligations in order to avoid physical annihilation, they are also very much aware of the danger of cultural annihilation through assimilation with the numerically dominant Hausa-speaking peoples. To Fulɓe cultural and physical annihilation are synonymous. They are clearly aware of the fact that if, for any reason, they lose their cattle, their cultural and ethnic identity will in due course be lost, and they illustrate this fact by pointing out Fulɓe *siire* (former pastoralists) who are now intermarrying among the Haaɓe, and who for social purposes have 'become Haaɓe'. Quite apart from their economic value it would be almost impossible to overstress the symbolic importance of cattle in their integrative aspect. Ownership of cattle gives membership in the society and their loss results in expulsion. Membership in the society places an individual under the obligation to live according to a strict code of conduct (Fulfulde). Serious breaches of this code are believed to cause a reduction in the fertility and milk yield as well as an increase in the mortality of the herd upon which the offender is dependent.

A short Fulɓe metaphor, given here in free translation, expresses in a bovine idiom the way in which they visualize their society. They compare living persons to a herd of cattle which are moving down a straight road. The road (Fulɓe values, Fulfulde) has been given to them by their ancestors and should be regarded as sacred. The 'cattle' should not deviate from the road which has been given to them. They go on to say that every herd should have a leader and it is the duty of the herd to follow that leader. However, it is recognized that in any herd there are always those cattle who do not follow the leader well and may stray from the road, eventually however, to rejoin the herd. But there are always, unfortunately, a few cattle which stray badly and may ultimately be lost—which is tragic but inevitable.

It may now be appreciated that individually and collectively (as a society) the Fulɓe feel extremely insecure. They rightly recognize that their fortunes both individually and as a group are dependent upon the degree to which they are able to maintain or increase their herds through the years. They have learnt from long experience in an unkindly habitat that it takes many years of applied skill and industry to build up a sizeable herd, but only a very short time with bad luck or poor judgement for the herd to decrease or be lost.

A man's first ambition is to own cattle which are his claim to membership in the society. The degree to which he subsequently gains status and prestige will largely depend upon how successful he is in helping to perpetuate the Fulɓe society as a distinctive ecological, ethnic, and cultural group, that is by maintaining (or preferably increasing) the numbers of his cattle, by observing Fulɓe *na'i* endogamy in his marriages, by producing children and by living according to the ethical standards of Fulfulde. A man with few cattle has little status, but a man with no cattle at all is rejected by his society and deprived of his privileged status of 'being a Pullo'.

5

PATTERNS OF TRANSHUMANCE

THE purpose of this section is to indicate some of the more important aspects of the annual cycle of movements followed by the Fulɓe and their herds. Primarily their transhumance may be viewed as an ecological adaptation, the object of which is to secure the best conditions for the herds in the varying physio-climatic conditions found in the yearly cycle. The movement of the herds and their keepers cannot be regarded as due to a 'restless spirit' or any other similar personality trait of the Fulɓe which compels them to move at intervals. Indeed they prefer to live under conditions which are so favourable to their needs that long moves are not necessary. But, as their life centres around their herds, they feel obliged and eager to take them where they will fare the best.

For our area the basic movement is down to the Sokoto River valley flood-plain and southwards in the dry season, and to the upland bush and northward in the wet season. While some Gwandu Fulɓe do not find it necessary to move to the south each year, as movement along a line running east and west from the river to the upland bush provides adequate pasture, as a rule, the south to north movement in the wet season and the north to south movement in the dry season are typical wherever pastoral nomads are found in the Western Sudan, being linked with the decrease of rainfall as one moves towards the desert. Accordingly, in our area too, once the dry season is well in progress there is a steady flow of herds down the Sokoto River valley moving towards the Niger.

While the Fulɓe give their primary interest to their cattle, their herds are not always of sufficient size for them to be entirely pastoral as they would prefer. They have a strong contempt for farming as an occupation and whenever they can afford it and can find Haaɓe labourers, they will hire them to do the work. There is no clear-cut correlation between the size of a man's herd and his disposition to farm; that is, herdsmen with comparatively large herds may have farms, while those with relatively small herds may not farm at all. Obviously, if a man has only a small number of cattle he will have to farm, but a man with more than 100 head of cattle (a large herd) may also farm. In addition to the size of a man's herd (and hence his income) there are many factors which incline a household head to farm or not, and these vary to some extent locally. In some areas the price of milk fluctuates widely and corn may not be available at a reasonable price, so that herd-owners are compelled to grow at least a portion of their own grain requirements. Cattle husbandry is a hazardous occupation and it is faced with more confidence by some than by others. The more cautious practise farming in order to guard against the risk. Some herdsmen are very confident about their ability in cattle husbandry and, apart from trying to improve their status, feel that if they do not farm they will benefit by their greater mobility and ultimately the herd will prosper. There are those who would like to farm but cannot spare the personnel nor find Haaɓe wage-labour. In deciding whether to farm or not, a man's personal idiosyncracies play a large part: some people are more ambitious than others; there are variations in the amount of hardship which individuals are prepared to withstand, and some men are driven to take up farming by their wives who continually complain that they cannot provide enough food for the household from the returns from the sale of milk.

The necessity for farming is basically economic, but in all cases a number of other factors contribute to the making of the choice. In a random sample of 100 family households in southern Gwandu it was found that 66 supplemented their incomes by farming. Only a very small percentage raise cash crops; when corn is grown it is used for domestic consumption.

Except among those Fulɓe who are unusually poor in cattle, *gero* (bulrush millet) is the crop which is generally grown. From the pastoralist's point of view this crop has the advantage of early maturity (82 days after planting, according to one instance observed) which means that the members of the household are not kept from their cattle as long as they would be if they grew the later maturing varieties of corn or engaged in the production of a diversity of crops. Another important point is that *gero* thrives on upland soil which is not in short supply. Farming on a small scale as they do, the Fulɓe do not require an established residence in a village, which is an advantage to them.

The pastoral population may be placed in three economic categories:

1. Those Fulɓe who do not farm.
2. Those who have enough cattle to maintain a subsistence level only if they grow small plots of *gero*.
3. Those who have so few cattle that they must grow a diversity of crops including *gero*, guinea corn, rice, groundnuts, and beans.

This classification is admittedly arbitrary, for there are, as we have seen, a number of complicating variables and there is some overlapping between the categories. Group 1 forms a small percentage of the population and, at any given time, will include family households which farmed a year or two previously but were not farming at the moment of the inquiry. They may have recently abandoned farming because they have changed the orbit of their movement, or because the size of their household, owing to some crisis, has changed, or there has been an increase in the herd, or for one of many other reasons. Only a small percentage, indeed, of group 1 have never farmed within their memory.

Group 2 is the most important category numerically. Growing *gero* is an encumbrance, but not so great as seriously to interfere with a workable system of transhumance. Since *gero* matures quickly on land which is not in short supply, and since a fixed residence is not necessary for its cultivation, the system practised by group 2 is flexible. The farm is usually located in the dry-season grazing area so that the grain is available when the domestic need is greatest—the milk yield being lowest in the dry season. Moreover, since *gero* is planted early in the wet season, it is often possible to harvest it before the cattle are moved to the wet-season area. This is an important point for, with the family household as an economic unit, efficiency is lost and hardship is increased when such a small unit is dispersed.

Group 3 is a category the members of which are, in the economic sense, similar to the Haaɓe. Their cash income is mainly derived from farm produce and the necessary diversity means that they are not free to follow the cattle; they must acquire a compound and live more or less permanently in a village and either send their cattle off with friends or kin or keep them near their village under relatively unfavourable grazing conditions. Fulɓe of group 3 are in a critical position for, in time, they are likely either to become Fulɓe *siire* or, if they prosper, to enter or re-enter group 2.

The fact that Fulɓe of Gwandu Emirate must farm is of considerable significance in the understanding of transhumance, for it implies that not only must certain members of the household be occupied seasonally on farm work, but also the herd must spend a considerable portion of the year near the farm in order that advantage may be taken by household members of the domestic grain supply. If the domestic labour force permits, *gero* may be carried (by men usually with donkeys) up to 15 miles from the storage bin to the cattle camp. But moving *gero* a long distance when the labour supply is limited, as it often is, is inconvenient and it is more usual to sell the corn in or near the village in which it is stored and with the proceeds buy near the camp.

Now there is, of course, considerable variation in the distances between the extreme points covered by the various herds in their annual travel. In a recent study of pastoral movements in western Sokoto Province it was found that out of a sample of 63 'groups' the average one way distance covered was 73 miles.[1] The frequency distribution was as follows:

No. of miles	No. of 'groups'
0 to 19	8
20 „ 39	8
40 „ 59	8
60 „ 79	19
80 „ 99	3
100 „ 119	3
120 and over	14
Total	63

Estimated minimum 6 miles; estimated maximum 188 miles.

Many of the Fulɓe in the sample were in Gwandu Emirate in the dry season, but if we consider only those Fulɓe who hold farms in Gwandu (or consider Gwandu to be their 'home') then the distances covered are on the average less.

To the casual observer the periodic movement of the herdsmen and their cattle appears as a routine task which is conducted without much thought or foresight. But moves are made only after considering an infinite variety of factors and after a series of deliberations which, in the case of more important moves, may have

[1] C. Hanson-Smith, op. cit.

PLATE I

a. A mother and her daughter grind corn. In the background is their dry-season
wind-screen with domestic utensils

Photo. Dr. N. A. Barnicot

b. A young mother and her son

Photo. Dr. N. A. Barnicot

PLATE II

a. In the late dry season swimming herdsmen guide their cattle across the Niger in search of better pastures

b. A herd-boy passes the long and lonely hours in playing his flute

Photo. Dr. N. A. Barnicot

begun weeks before the migration. Yet, in an emergency, a camp may move at about an hour's notice. A detailed knowledge of their area, a remarkable skill in cattle husbandry, and an efficient organization of the household and camp make it possible for the Fulɓe to make effective plans in advance and also to act quickly should the occasion demand it.

The life of the pastoralist requires a series of annual rhythmic movements occasioned by the sharp climatic dichotomy of the dry and the wet seasons. Fulɓe divide the year into five seasons, each of which has a distinctive type of weather. The names and characteristics of these seasons, as well as the terms[1] used to denote the area in which the season was spent, are given below.

Dungu (*rumirde*). The wet season proper which begins late in June or during July and ends late in September or early in October (3–4 months).

'*Yawal* ('*yawirde*). The hot season after the rains. This begins late in October and ends about the end of December (1–1½ months).

Ɗabunde (*ɗabirde*). The season of the Harmattan—cool dry season from December to February inclusive (3 months).

Cheedu (*chedirde*). The hot season after the Harmattan. The beginning and ending varies as do the other seasons. It begins late in February or early in March and ends about the latter part of April (2 months).

Seeto (*setinirde*). The windy and stormy period leading into the rains. From early May until into June (1–1½ months).

We must now briefly consider what is entailed at the various seasonal sites from the point of view of those who depend on their herds for their subsistence. We begin with the *rumirde*.

A. *Rumirde*

The wet season is a time during which, despite many hardships, morale is high. Pastoralists feel immensely relieved to find an abundance of pastures once again. Day by day they see their cattle gaining weight and increasing their yield of milk in response to the lush grazing. Although it may not be expressed, a herdsman feels some pride in the fact that his herd has survived another dry season. Fulɓe walk through the woods for ten or more miles to the scattered bush villages where they may meet several hundred others who are spending the wet season in the same area and many

---

[1] With one exception, these are derived from the names of the seasons.

of whom may not have met for a year or more. This is the time when solidarity is at its height for now, being in great numbers, they feel that they are an important minority in the Hausa-speaking community and it is a great pleasure to be with one's own kind.

The wet season is regarded as the most pleasant time of the year for the Fulɓe, but even at this time there are enough problems to restrain exuberance: '*dungu kanjum woni beldum amma torra i don*' (lit. 'the wet season is a pleasant time but there is hardship'). It is an index of the affection that Fulɓe cherish for their cattle that they do not complain seriously of the physical hardships of their lives during the wet season, of getting wet and cold. Despite the abundance of pasture camps are moved quite regularly during the rains. There are various reasons for this:

1. If the cattle stay at one site for a long time, the ground, being wet, becomes soggy, and there is said to be a danger of bovine foot infection; also, flies become a menace.
2. By moving frequently there is an opportunity to graze the best grasses, thus getting the herd into the best possible physical condition to withstand the next dry season. Frequent moves ensure that good grass is within a few yards of the camp and the animals can browse whenever they feel the need.
3. The cattle-tax (*jangal*) is collected in the wet season. Frequent moves increase the possibility of escaping the collector.

For these reasons camps may move, on an average, every three to ten days and in these circumstances shelters of even the most elementary kind are not erected. A pile of herbage is laid on the ground and on top of this a sleeping mat is placed; another sleeping mat over the individual is intended to deflect the rain from above while the pile of grass and the mat underneath serve to prevent seepage from below. This type of *dungu* shelter is only moderately successful, the result of which is many sleepless nights.

Some Fulɓe endeavour to reduce the hardship of the *dungu*, for some at least of the camp members, by building waterproof 'bee-hive' shelters of grass and saplings (*bukaaru*, pl. *bukaaji*) which are clear of the farmed areas. Having built their shelters, the household herds are divided roughly in half, one segment remaining near the shelters while the other is herded by youths who, travelling without encumbrances, can seek out the best pastures and have a good chance of escaping should they be involved in trouble caused by crop damage. *Jangal* (cattle-tax) may be paid on the cattle at the fixed camp and the receipt may be 'juggled' as required between the segments of the divided herd. This type of *rumirde* camp organization is called *ɓigal*.[1]

The decision as to where and when to move in the *rumirde* (as in other seasons), although anticipated with some pleasure, is not made without carefully weighing a series of ecological, political, social, and economic questions. The element of choice lies in the fact that each herd-owner must choose one *rumirde* out of several. With respect to the time of a move and the place to which to move, decisions are based not only on a detailed knowledge of a wide area, but also on elaborate information which is gathered as the time for the move approaches.

European and Haaɓe observers frequently comment on the indolence of the Fulɓe who are invariably seen in numbers in the markets of the area pastured by their herds. But in the present context much significance can be attached to the Fulɓe statement: *'mi do yiddi yahugo luumo gam mi hebbai habaru dunyaru'* (lit. 'I like to go to the market because I hear news of the world'); for the Fulɓe the market is a clearing house for a vast store of detailed information which is vital to them in their pastoral existence. Seen on the ground, markets may be visualized as the centres of a series of overlapping circles through which information is circulated and which provide an amazing means of mass communication.[2] The great attraction of the markets is seen in the fact that it is exceptional to find adult men in the camps during the day. Occasionally one may see an able-bodied man in a camp after his fellows have gone to the village, but this may mean that he has been detained in some task and is likely to go later in the day.

Owners leave the camp a few minutes after the herds have gone to the pastures in the morning and return just before the cattle come back in the evening. According to the season and the distance of the camp from the village, the men spend from three to nine hours in the markets, during which time they have long chats with

---

[1] The derivation of this term is obscure. It may come from the radical *ɓi* in 'child' (*ɓiddo*, pl. *ɓiɓɓe*), for the cattle are in the charge of the youths. The first type of camp organization mentioned above does not have a special name.

[2] An illustration of this point can be drawn from my own experience. On one occasion I bought a horse and immediately thereafter I set out on a fifty-mile trek. When I arrived at my destination (in advance of my domestics) I was not surprised to learn that the Fulɓe knew where I bought the horse and exactly how much I had paid for it.

their friends and kin who may be camped elsewhere. They also take the opportunity to overhear conversations in which they are not themselves engaged.[1] Since Fulɓe men generally have friends, not only in their own camps but also in the camps of others, the amount of information which finds its way back to the camps in the evening is very considerable. The most vital type of data gathered from the market sources is the kind which is most variable, such as the present quality of the pasture-lands, the availability of water, whether the traditional routes remain open or whether they have been farmed over. Up-to-date information is also required on the presence or absence of endemic bovine diseases, and the number of flies and mosquitoes. They like also to obtain data on the whereabouts of lions and hyenas.[2]

The actual move to the *rumirde* begins in July when the pastures of the riverain areas begin to deteriorate and the upland bush grazing improves. However, it is not until August, when the *gero* is harvested, that the herds are found in great numbers in the upland bush. Very often the first to reach the *rumirde* are cattle-owners who do not farm at all or, if they do farm, have left people behind to work on the land or to supervise the Haaɓe wage-labour. Fulɓe who enter the *rumirde* after the *gero* harvest leave their cattle at a camp in the bush about a mile or more from the farm during the growing season and the harvest.

For those who are the first to enter the *rumirde* there is the advantage of greater mobility for the herd for a larger portion of the *dungu*. Those who camp near their farms early in the *dungu* have less mobility and the danger of their causing crop damage is somewhat greater, but they have the advantage of being able to rely on their own supply of *gero* from the previous harvest.

The principal ecological feature of the *dungu* is the abundance of

---

[1] All Gwandu Fulɓe adults speak Hausa although some of them know it imperfectly. Children first learn Fulfulde but, as their sphere of activities begins to extend beyond the camp, they gradually learn Hausa.

[2] Informants have given up favoured grazing areas because of fear of lions and hyenas or actual cattle mortality through attacks. Some Fulɓe have a *magani ladde* (bush medicine) which is a spitting charm and is thought to be effective in preventing the approach of predatory beasts. Since attacks from lions and hyenas are normally nocturnal, poison arrows and swords are of little use. Lions are not so numerous as to be a serious menace, but the same cannot be said of the hyenas which are both numerous and widely dispersed. Hyenas frequently mutilate and kill stock and, in addition, they are a hazard for they create anxiety and cause the cattle to expend much valuable energy in stampeding to escape attack.

pasture of high quality. From the point of view of the welfare of the herd, the object is to fatten the cattle as much as possible so that they may survive the less favourable conditions at the end of the dry season.

Late in September the rainfall begins to lessen and, with the longer hours of sunshine, the grass begins to dry out and the surface water of the upland bush starts to evaporate: this marks the end of the *dungu*.

B. ' *Yawirde*

During October, owing to the deterioration of upland bush grazing and the decrease in the supply of water, the cattle are moved in the direction of the river valley once more, but they stop a few miles in the bush to await the first stubble grazing which becomes available in November. Strictly speaking, the *'yawirde* is neither wet- nor dry-season grazing, for at this time they rely first on the bush grazing and later on stubble grazing. This season, like *dungu*, calls for careful grazing in order to avoid damage to the standing crops. In *'yawal* the surface water supply of the upland bush is not adequate for the maintenance of the herds and, in addition, the herdsmen wish to be near at hand to take the best of the stubble grazing which is available after the harvest.

The period of *'yawal* ends when the Harmattan season begins in December or late November.

c. *Dabirde*

Early in *dabunde* the late maturing varieties of corn are completely harvested and again the herds are free to camp on the farm-lands which surround the villages. Stubble is often grazed by herds which are on the move to the farm area of the cattle-owner. The *dabunde* lasts from December until late February or early March. During this period the Fulɓe return to their own farm area, going first to the farm-lands of the village and district heads where they corral their cattle for about ten nights. A village or district head may give gifts of kola-nuts to the herd-owners who keep their cattle on his farm-lands, but the herdsmen do not expect further remuneration.

After having manured the farm of the local chief the pastoralists disperse to other farms within the same village area, keeping their cattle on each farm for periods which may vary from three to ten nights. No fixed fee is charged for corralling the cattle on the farm of a peasant farmer. Herd-owners are quite pleased if they receive enough corn for their domestic needs while they are on a farm and they may or may not receive kola-nuts and possibly salt in addition. If any remuneration is paid in cash, the amount is established by bargaining before the herd is moved on to the farm. Herd-owners whose cattle are in transit and spend one night on a farm do not receive payment from the farm-owner.

At some stage in the dry season a herdsman will use his cattle to manure his own farm if he has one.

The *ɗabunde* is a season of progressive decline in the condition of the pastures. As grazing deteriorates pastoralists abandon the possibility of gaining an income from manuring and give priority to seeking out the best pastures. They may move to the middle of the flood-plain of the Sokoto River (in places where the valley is wide) and thus increase the radius of flood-land grazing rather than obtain income from manuring the upland farms.

Shelters in the *ɗabunde* reflect the necessity of frequent moves, for they are simple wind-screens built for the protection of the light calabashes and used also to provide shade for women and children.

The comparatively cool weather of the *ɗabunde* changes, when the Harmattan ends, into the *cheedu*—the late dry season.

D. *Chedirde*

The main feature of this season is the deterioration of grazing conditions to which the Fulɓe again adapt their ecological techniques. There is a pervasive atmosphere of depression reflected in short tempers and dejected spirits, although there is an attempt to be agreeable if not cheerful outside one's own household. The population is lethargic for with little milk, practically all of which is used for the calves, some households have no nourishment but corn broth and practically all admit to hunger even immediately after meals. At this season Fulɓe are poor informants for they prefer to sleep, remain silent, or discuss only the most urgent business.

Southerly movements are at a maximum at this season as cattle move to the banks of the Niger for the best grazing. In some cases entire households may move or a household may be split up. Some Fulɓe are afraid to go to the Niger because of the risk of cattle mortality through liver-fluke which appears to have a higher incidence there than along the Sokoto River. Other herd-owners are afraid to go to the Niger owing to a vague general fear of the river due to unfamiliarity.

It should be mentioned that, apart from the deterioration caused by the natural conditions of seasonal drought and strong sunshine, pastures are destroyed on an appreciable scale by fires set by the Haaɓe. Fulɓe say that the Haaɓe burn the dry grass out of malice towards the Fulɓe and their cattle. The Haaɓe themselves say that they burn rice stubble in order to make pre-planting cultivation easier and they burn upland grasses in hunting. However, the result of the fires is that, apart from increasing upland erosion, as has been noted, hundreds of square miles of pasture are destroyed precisely when they are most urgently needed.

E. *Setinirde*

In this season the rain returns and is followed almost immediately by fresh grass shoots which begin to cover the large tracts of what was until recently sandy wastes broken by stretches of dry grass. When planting begins herds are moved clear of the farms. They may stay for a time on the islands of the Niger or on the higher ground of the Sokoto River flood-plain. Ideally this site is within 2 or 3 miles of the farm so that the herd can be attended to and the farm worked from the same homestead. The detailed arrangements may vary considerably with the area and from year to year. Pastoralists without farms are free to move to wet-season grazing without concerning themselves with cultivation and harvest, and it is here that they have an advantage over those who farm.

It is appreciated that the above description of Fulɓe ecology and transhumance is highly generalized. But since space is limited it has been necessary to condense this section to the minimum required for an understanding of the sociological data and analysis which follow.

SECTION II

6

THE GWANDU FULƁE DURING THE 'TIME OF WAR'

ALTHOUGH a detailed analysis of the process of social change is not attempted here it is necessary, before we discuss the family and its herd, to give a brief outline of the pastoral society during what the Fulɓe themselves call the 'Time of War' (*zammanu gaaba*)—the period immediately before the British conquest in 1903. To further the understanding of the modern society certain post-Protectorate changes are also discussed below under the heading of the 'Period of Transition'.

The information on the 'Time of War' is based on statements given by elderly informants. Unfortunately, however, owing to the length of time that has elapsed since the conquest, the information obtained was not sufficiently detailed, or susceptible of verification, to enable a detailed reconstruction to be made. In addition, as has been said, after the conquest many Fulɓe of the clan-villages dispersed and intermingled in areas which were new to them. Thus pastoralists living within a given village area had come from different clans and from widely separated areas. Today, herdsmen of such heterogeneous village areas do not, as a rule, attempt to learn or remember the minutiae of traditions or the 'history' of their own clan, but instead there is a tendency to reduce the 'history' of local pastoralists to, as it were, the lowest common denominator so that they all share a generalized but similar background.

Data collected from informants have an internal consistency and are in general agreement when concerned with those aspects which are documented. The outline of the 'Time of War' which follows is the way in which the Fulɓe view the past, and it is, in our opinion, a reasonably accurate account of the social and political reality of the period immediately preceding the Protectorate.

During the nineteenth century the Fulɓe lived in or near walled endogamous clan-villages along with their slaves, or slaves and subject peoples. The slaves farmed the area immediately surrounding the wall and the cattle grazed the area round the perimeter of the cultivated land. Gwandu Fulɓe still have a vivid memory of the frequent raiding by the Kebbi forces during the nineteenth century (see p. 16). Informants often mention the fact that only the able-bodied men and youths (Fulɓe and slave) attended to the cattle in the 'Time of War', for only the physically vigorous could hope to deal effectively with the surprise attacks. Herd attendants along with their cattle then chose either to escape to the depths of the bush or to drive the cattle within the walls of the village.

One might visualize the countryside of Gwandu during the 'Time of War' as consisting of a series of walled clan-villages (sometimes interspersed among purely Haaɓe villages) located at intervals of from 5 to 15 or more miles from each other. Around such villages cultivation could be both permanent and intensive owing to regular manuring by Fulɓe herds. Beyond the perimeter of the farmland was virgin bush which extended without interruption to the farm-lands of the next village. Cattle were grazed on the edge of the bush near the village. Herdsmen say that in those days the pastoralists tolerated rather indifferent conditions of pasturage, not because there was a shortage of grass and water in Gwandu country as a whole, but because the herd-owners were afraid to move their cattle far from the village. Because herd-owners were thus effectively tied to specific villages there appears to have been little inter-clan conflict over grazing lands within what is now Gwandu Emirate, although pastoralists from Kebbi frequently captured cattle from what is now western Sokoto and Gwandu Emirates.

The walls of the villages, which were allowed to fall into disrepair shortly after the pacification, are of interest to us since they provide a crude basis for estimating the population in the old days. The walls were built of sun-baked earth. The earth was excavated from a trench which acted as a moat when the wall had been erected. The strength of the walls varied to some extent according to the size of the labour force available to build them, but we may estimate that even for a wall around one of the smaller villages (a perimeter of a mile or so) a labour force of several hundred men working for at least six months would be required. Calculations as to the village population based on the area surrounded by the wall are not easily made, since we have no way of knowing the density within the wall nor do we know precisely the Fulɓe-Haaɓe ratio. But by comparing the area surrounded by the walls and the same area of habitation today (for which we have reasonably accurate census figures) we may estimate that the population varied from a minimum of about 500 to a few thousand individuals. Of this number probably from 200 to 600, according to the size of the village, were Fulɓe.[1]

In view of the conditions of insecurity, which called for strongly developed corporate activities for defence, we can accept the Fulɓe view that there was an intense sense of solidarity among the Fulɓe members of the clan-village: '*denno Fulɓe nder lenyol ɓe kewi sumpo*' (lit. 'then the Fulɓe of the clan had much solidarity'). The clan-village was a closed, largely endogamous group and membership was dependent on birth.[2] Fulɓe attribute the solidarity of their ancestors in the clan-village to the fact that they were all of common origin and they say, 'does one not like a person who has the same ancestor as oneself'. Provisionally we may attribute this solidarity to the fact that the village existed in virtual isolation in a hostile world; support by other villages, owing to their spatial separation and the fact that raids were by surprise, could not be relied on, and the members were united in a common objective of defence against their enemies.

Although the clan (*lenyol*, pl. *le'i*) has little functional significance today, informants have, generally speaking, a very uniform impression as to its broad features during the 'Time of War'. The

[1] In support of the demographic inferences made above it should be noted that informants hold that in the clan-village the Fulɓe were always considerably in the minority as a group. Pasture for cattle, upon which Fulɓe were ultimately dependent, was a limiting factor in local Fulɓe density. Slaves, on the other hand, according to the informants, were always a glut in the market since a proportion of the tribute paid to Gwandu from outlying states was slaves.

[2] Field evidence suggests, however, that near Sokoto the exclusiveness of the clans was not so pronounced, since the local Fulɓe population was made up of a series of splinter-groups who were said to have come in order to be 'near Shefu'. These Fulɓe intermingled freely in the Sokoto market-place and at the mosque. It seems likely that in these circumstances inter-clan friendships were formed and that these were followed by marriage—the latter point is, however, strongly denied by the informants. It should be noted also that Shefu appears to have been aware of the exclusiveness of the clans and it is said that he urged the Fulɓe to suppress their clan rivalries in the interests of Islam and a peaceful community. Informants hold that his counsel had little effect outside the immediate environs of Sokoto.

men, women, and children of a clan claimed to have descended through males from a common male ancestor. The degree to which the members of a clan were genealogically knowledgeable in the past is obscure; but today it is uncommon to trace descent back for more than three generations from adults. However, it seems likely that in the past people were much more aware of their genealogies than they are today, for the dispersal of the clan has made it more difficult for an individual to learn the details of his genealogy and also, in modern conditions, such knowledge has little practical value. It is probable that in the past the name of the founding ancestor of a clan was known, but today this is rarely the case. The belief that the members of a clan also had a common unnamed ancestress is variously expressed by saying that members of a clan were of one shelter (*suudu*, each wife being allocated a separate shelter), one womb (*reedu*), or one umbilical cord (*wudu*).

For the purpose of identification members of a given clan very often, but by no means always, adopted the name of the village at or near which they had lived for at least a generation. Thus, for example, the Fulɓe who lived at Gwomba (Kaoji District) during the 'Time of War' referred to themselves as Gwombanko'en (lit. the peoples of Gwomba).

The clan was under the leadership of the senior member of the senior line, but succession was subject to the approval of the elders of the clan. Failing a suitable son (either because of his being too young or because of personal disqualifications), the leader (usually called *Sarkin* (H.) or *Lamiiɗo* (F.)) could be succeeded by his most senior brother.[1] After having gained the approval of the elders of the clan the new leader, if accepted by the Sarkin Gwandu, would receive ceremonially a gown and turban from the latter.

The leader had few privileges and dared not flout the views of his following. He was shown respect in virtue of the fact that he was recognized by the head of the Gwandu Empire; he enjoyed popular approval and he symbolized the unity of the local group. But he was still a kinsman to the members of the village and he was required to fulfil the associated obligations, little latitude being given because of his office.

Since, as we have seen, the Fulɓe local group was small and the

---

[1] In the past, as today, seniority was reckoned according to the order of birth without reference to the order of marriage of the wives, although there is a feeling that a man should not marry a second wife until his first wife has borne him a son.

clan homogeneous, the sanction of public opinion was generally effective in social control and produced a high degree of conformity in day-to-day behaviour. In minor cases of anti-social behaviour, for example, failure to show respect towards an elder, the offender would find that Fulɓe villagers would refuse to speak to him or co-operate with him until he had formally repented. For a more serious offence (for example, illicit sexual intercourse) the leader could, with the approval of the elders, sentence the offender to exile. Thus the main instrument of social control rested on the desire of the clan members to preserve the respect of their fellows in their clan-village. Respect was acquired largely, but not exclusively, according to an individual's excellence in living up to the strict ethical standards (*fulfulde*) of the society. For relatively minor breaches of the ethical standards, respect and ultimately co-operation were forfeited. But a sanction of even greater force was the revocation of clan membership from an individual whose right it was by birth. The strength of this sanction lay in the fact that an individual could claim the right to live in only one village. To risk the loss of this right was unthinkable, for a man who was rejected by his own clan faced a world in which he would be treated with suspicion if not with hostility.

The nature of extra-village relations of course varied locally, for Gwandu Emirate covers a wide area. In principle a clan head had to report serious crimes such, for example, as homicide, to the *alkali's* court at Gwandu. A clan head was also obliged to keep the peace in his own village and to maintain friendly relations with other villages which owed allegiance to Gwandu. But Gwandu was often so preoccupied with holding its own against Kebbi and with problems of administration in the wider Empire that it was not free to supervise the home districts closely or to curtail their freedom. Especially when Gwandu could trust the loyalty of its hinterland chiefs there was little interference with village administration. It is said by some informants that Gwandu was so lax that some villages paid their tithes, which in theory should have been paid annually, only once every two or three years. A proportion of clan-villages did not feel that they were obliged to pay tithes, for while they had formally given allegiance to Gwandu, they had received little protection and were responsible for their own defence. However, to some extent the title to office given to the clan heads by the Emir of Gwandu did promote a sense of unity among those villages which had accepted the formal suzerainty of the Sarkin Gwandu as the head of the State. Thus, while in many cases Gwandu did not interfere directly in village administration, its indirect influence as a symbol of the wider Moslem community did in turn influence the relations between villages in the State, and their hostility was projected towards the enemies of Islam—Kebbi to the west and, to a smaller extent, Bussa and Illo to the south.

Because of the persistence of raids and threats of raids, particularly from Kebbi, social contact between villages was severely limited and Fulɓe say that there was little inter-village co-operation in offensive or defensive action against enemies. Because raids were by surprise and of short duration there was little opportunity for collective defence among villages.

The fact that a village depended on a wall for its defences meant that the local group was comparatively large. In these circumstances individuals or small groups of Fulɓe and their slaves could not move off at random. A common practice in response to population growth was for the original wall to be extended or a new wall of greater circumference to be built—in some cases traces of successive walls still remain. In other instances, when the population grew, a large group of Fulɓe and their slaves would hive-off and, in an area suitable both for farming and for grazing, they would build a new walled village. The nature of the political and social relations between the old and the new village varied according to the circumstances in which the cleavage came about.

Comparatively small groups building a village within a few miles of the parent village tended to remain under their former chief and pay their tithes through him. Other, generally larger, groups might move farther off and appeal directly to Gwandu for recognition of status independent of the parent village. The spatial distance which separated the old and the new village was often an index of the social distance between the two groups after their cleavage.

While it is clear that from time to time some members of a clan-village would hive-off and settle elsewhere, informants were emphatic that the clan was not internally segmented as a regular structural feature. But whether or not the clan structure emerged only with the political changes following the Jihad movement must, because of insufficient evidence, remain an open question. However, regardless of the details of pre-Jihad structure, on theoretical grounds it would appear that a clan-type local organization was functionally congenial to the political reality of the 'Time of War'. For it will be remembered that the Fulɓe were in a pivotal position between Haaɓe enemies on the one hand and the Gwandu capital on the other. In this setting, Fulɓe of a village could best serve their own interests by acting as a strongly corporate unit on all issues.

We have said that the clan-village was endogamous. While Fulɓe say that they have 'always' been averse to marrying Haaɓe or taking them as concubines, it is clear that in certain cases, when there was a marked difference in the numbers of marriageable males and females, the difficulty could be overcome by men taking Haaɓe slaves as concubines. For this was recognized as better than remaining without a sexual partner. The fact that female slaves could easily be purchased in the markets (as also could men) thus served, when necessary, to preserve local endogamy and also to reduce tension among men arising over competition for marriageable women. Children of concubines, be it noted, enjoyed full legal status although they suffered a degree of social stigma; for social status is, to some extent, linked with the lightness of one's skin —comparatively light skin being a racial characteristic of which the pastoralists are extremely proud.

In summary, the fact that villages were largely autonomous and also isolated, both physically and socially, gave the intra-village relations a special character. The solidarity attributed to the unit by informants may well be exaggerated, but they do mention certain features of social life which suggest a marked solidarity. For example, it is said that any marriage or divorce was not only an important event to the close kin of the spouses, but was also to some extent the concern of all Fulɓe of the village. It is also said that if a man did not have enough cattle for his domestic needs his kinsmen or clansmen would lend him the cattle which he required. Even minor disputes between individuals were recognized as potentially disruptive of solidarity and the elders are said to have acted quickly to attempt to settle differences.

Generally speaking, on the basis of much evidence, the interests of the individual and the family were, and had to be, subordinated to the wider interests of the clan-village as a whole if its corporate character, so necessary for its survival, was to be maintained.

The British pacification of Gwandu and Kebbi in 1902 and of Sokoto in 1903 brought striking changes in the society. It is our task now to show how some of the more important of these changes came about.

7

THE PERIOD OF TRANSITION

THE social change which followed the British conquest did not come about, as in many other societies in Africa, as a result of direct influences from media of Western culture contact such as the church and schools. In a general sense the Islamic community in Northern Nigeria, of which the Fulɓe are a part, has shown a strong resistance to the assimilation of Western ideals and institutions. And within this community the Fulɓe have been credited, as a people, with offering the strongest resistance to culture change. Scholars have long observed that pastoral peoples in general tend to have social systems which do not react quickly to alien stimulation. Nevertheless, it is clear that the Fulɓe society has undergone, and is still undergoing, a marked process of adaptation to the politico-ecological circumstances occasioned by the establishment of the Protectorate. While not neglecting the obvious complexity of all culture change processes, it is necessary to stress the importance, from the point of view of this analysis, of the security which followed the British conquest.

In this section an attempt is made to indicate the manner in which the clan as a social group has lost much of its former significance and also how the simple and polygynous family has emerged as a unit occupying a position of importance which was not characteristic in the past. In the modern society the social function of the clan is seen to vary from area to area and from context to context, but in no case can its function be regarded as equivalent to that which existed in earlier times. The Fulɓe, living in close symbiosis with the Haaɓe,[1] have a social system which, although maintaining some distinctiveness has, nevertheless, been sensitive to political fortunes and changes within the wider Hausa-speaking community. Our task now is to describe the way in which, in the context of the total Mohammedan community, the pastoral society has changed in the present century.

The conquest by the British forces impressed the Fulɓe and the

[1] A note on the nature and degree of symbiosis in the past and today is given below (see pp. 151-3).

Haaɓe alike with the 'strength' of the 'Europeans'. Less than a year after Sokoto was taken Haaɓe and Fulɓe alike began to move out of their fortified and overcrowded villages. As confidence in the new Administration grew, more and more people moved off in search of better farm-lands and pastures. The Fulɓe came to admire the British sense of 'justice' and from early times they had the impression that the administration would be secure and would stay for some time.

But having had their herds reduced by the rinderpest epidemic (1887–91) (p. 16) and, under British rule, having their slaves emancipated, the Fulɓe were in a difficult economic position. It was partly on account of the humiliation of living in a state of poverty in the same villages as their newly emancipated slaves, that some of the Fulɓe chose to move away from their traditional sites. Pastoralists with larger herds were in a position to take advantage of their new freedom, for they could live on the resources of the herd alone. Others with comparatively few cattle could move only if they left a segment of their household behind to farm. Still other herd-owners with even fewer cattle were obliged to stay near their traditional village, for the herds were not large enough to maintain their attendants. At their home village they began to farm alongside their emancipated slaves, gaining only a fraction of their subsistence from their cattle. Some were able to increase their herds and leave in search of better pastures to the south. Others, whose herds did not increase, or whose cattle died, remained at their traditional villages.

In the first years the most urgent problems facing the Administration were the suppression of slave traffic, the establishment of an equitable and efficient system of revenue collection to replace the tribute formerly paid to Sokoto and Gwandu by the States of the Empire, and the reform and systemization of the district administration. The various forms of taxes which had been imposed on practically all products and industries were abolished and replaced by a head-tax (*haraji*) and a cattle-tax (*jangali*) for the pastoralists.

The sub-division of the territory for administrative purposes was carried out along the lines of the best information available. Important villages became the centres of districts and less important villages were administered through them. In order to enforce Maliki Law over the whole territory and to assist in the policy of slave emancipation it was planned to have an *alkali* in each of the districts. The District Heads and *alkalis*[1] were to have limited authority in the executive and judicial spheres respectively.

The Administration, being as yet unfamiliar with the country, and also being grossly understaffed, was not in a position to learn the details of the social life of the elusive Fulɓe however valuable they might be as a source of revenue—if the tax were collected. While the Fulɓe took advantage of their freedom of movement not only to find the best grazing, but also to avoid the payment of cattle-tax. Having until recently relied for their subsistence on the crops grown by their slaves, their herds were scarcely adequate for their needs and this provided an active stimulus for their further movement.

The Haaɓe too reacted quickly to the new peaceful environment, for not only did the slave and subject peoples turn to the cultivation of virgin lands, but traders were able to travel at will without paying high taxes on their goods and without being escorted in large armed caravans. Pagans living in bush enclaves removed from the traditional trade routes could now obtain a wider range of goods than previously.

Reacting to the freedom of communications Islamic scribes and learned men (*modiibo*, pl. *modiiɓe*) began to cover a wider area in their travels carrying their influence beyond the large towns, the former centres of Mohammedan learning. The overall effect was a growing 'levelling' of the community—both Fulɓe and Haaɓe began to develop an interest in, and knowledge of, an area wider than their natal village.

A most important development following the conquest was that markets began to multiply and a much wider range of goods was available. Fulɓe now living in dispersed homesteads throughout the countryside looked to the markets not only as a means of trade but also as important social centres. Although they slept in their bush shelters near their cattle, adult men and women began to spend their days in the markets. Here they would meet their friends and kin, the women would sell their milk and butter and the men would gather information necessary for their seasonal pastoral movements. As a result of the visits to the markets cross-clan friendships were formed and these were followed by marriage. As ties with the traditional village began to grow weaker they were replaced by an

---

[1] I give the plural of Arabic and Hausa words by adding 's' to the singular.

interest in the new area. If a household head decided that a new village area was congenial to his needs he would ask the village head, if he desired, for farm-land in order to offset the economic risks in cattle husbandry or to increase his income.

Under the new system individual families (simple and poly-gynous) began to assume responsibility for their conduct without reference to their traditional leaders. Family heads themselves decided when or where to move or whether to remain in a given locality. No longer was an individual closely dependent upon a large corporate group to whom he could turn for co-operation or appeal in his own defence. The local *alkali*'s court became the centre to which he could appeal if serious offences were committed against him, and similarly he came to fear the *alkali* who might summons him if he were to commit delicts.

Following a similar pattern marriage became a matter which concerned a much narrower range of kin—both in the preliminary arrangements and in the crises of married life. Formerly the affines of both the spouses were resident in the same village and it is averred that they were active in settling marital disputes. Under the new system the pattern of residence continued to be either viri-local or neo-local, but a wife was often separated from her parents so that the conciliatory powers of the affines were weakened. Very often, as we shall see, the wife, in a marital dispute, came to have a weak bargaining position and, in her own defence, she had the choice of returning to her own kin or, if they lived too far away, appealing to the local *alkali*.

It should be noted also that the presence of the *alkali* at district headquarters served as an ultimate sanction in day-to-day Fulɓe affairs and Fulɓe say that with *alkalis* in the districts they have had to give up the severe beating of their wives and children as measures of discipline.[1] While beating may have been practised in the past, a man today will not beat his wife or children because he knows that if he does they will leave him. A youth has nothing to fear these days, for he knows that now he can either become a shepherd in Bornu or work for wages on the coast. On the other hand, a wife who is beaten will simply desert her husband. It is, however,

---

[1] Women who claim to have been mothers at the time of the conquest hold that wife-beating was a common practice in the 'Time of War' and in consequence wives, unlike those of today, were faithful to, and had 'respect' for, their husbands.

relevant to add that the *alkali* is greatly feared by the pastoralists. Since the *alkalis* are Haaɓe (or occasionally Fulɓe who have 'become' Haaɓe) they are thought to be strongly antipathetic to the herdsmen. So the *alkali* is feared as a person at whose hands a Pullo will suffer punishment rather than regarded as an official who will administer 'justice'.

In the 'Time of War' social control rested on the fact that the individuals of the clan-village put a high value on membership within the local group. The freedom of movement in the present century has destroyed the value of such membership and with it the effectiveness of the traditional sanctions. Persons who previously dared not risk forfeiting the support of clansmen and kinsmen were now free to control their own affairs and they could, and did, leave a local group on a trivial issue. In the absence of slaves a man came to depend very heavily on the co-operation of the members of his simple or polygynous family, for it was they who must attend to the routine tasks of gaining a livelihood. For help in emergencies a herd-owner began to seek the co-operation of friends (who were not necessarily clansmen or kinsmen) whom he had come to know in the market place. The terminology of clanship began to reflect the changed social reality, for the term for clansmen[1] began to be applied to all Fulɓe with whom a Pullo became acquainted.

This description of the changes which have taken place during the time of the Protectorate has deliberately been concise so as to reserve space for an account of the present-day society. In conclusion it should be mentioned that the process of change is still very active among the Fulɓe and they, being strongly 'ethno-conscious', are very much aware of the changes which are taking place. It is clear that the clan has lost most of its former significance and is being replaced, to some extent, by a sort of incipient local community. The centre of the new community is the village area, the inhabitants of which are not of a single clan but, having lived seasonally in the village hinterland for a number of years, have come to know and trust each other. In some areas, for example, the area occupied by the Jagadanko'en (lower Sokoto and Niger Rivers), ties of clanship still hold with a modicum of force, but even they admit that they are becoming like other Fulɓe with

---

[1] *bandirao*, pl. *bandiraaɓe*, from the root *bandu* meaning 'body'; hence, of the same body.

respect to the reduced significance of clanship. In general the individuals who tend to concern themselves least with the traditional values of the clan are strangers in a community who, in order to facilitate their own local integration, deny the value of maintaining clan sentiments. It is significant that elderly informants who have observed the process of change through the years say, 'today the Fulɓe are all one' (*hande Fulɓe fuh ɓe fuh ɓe go'o*) and the clan is no longer important. That clan affiliation is of minimal significance today is seen in the fact that while children of the age of about 4 years are clearly aware of the fact that they are Fulɓe, men and women up to the age of about 30 may not know the name of the clan of which they are members. In addition, some men who have been married for a number of years are not able to give the clan names of their wives. Generally speaking, the important thing today is being a Pullo and living correctly according to the rather rigid code which that implies. Individuals lay little stress on remembering the name of their clan and the traditions with which it is associated.

While the clan no longer exists as a co-residential, corporate unit, an important motive which Fulɓe have in describing the solidarity of the clan in the 'Time of War' is an attempt to transpose and perpetuate the same solidarity to some extent in the everyday life of today. More specifically, the behaviour of clansmen towards each other during the pre-Protectorate period is upheld as an ideal standard or charter. Fulɓe still think in terms of clans, but by a sort of fiction they endeavour to make the code of ethics (which was formerly binding only among the members of a clan) apply to all Fulɓe with whom they come in contact. There is a pervasive feeling among Fulɓe that as an ethnic and cultural group they face possible extinction under modern changing conditions and this, in itself, promotes a degree of solidarity which embraces all pastoralists regardless of clan affiliation.

The break-up of clans in the present century has necessarily been associated with changes in marriage as we shall see. For the present we need only state that traditional cousin marriage is declining in incidence, although its frequency is still considerable (see footnote, p. 80). One of the most important factors influencing the choice of spouses is locality, for if, for any reason, one clan is numerically dominant in a local community, cousin marriage among its members is likely to be high. When such marriages occur the motive may be to promote local solidarity by extending bonds of kinship and affinity, and thus discourage competition for pastures through the ingress of 'strangers'. Some Fulɓe, too, prefer to marry cousins for they feel that such unions are more likely to endure.

We turn now to a discussion of the family and its herd in the modern society.

8

THE FAMILY AND ITS HERD

THE basic social unit which enjoys a high degree of independence and is strongly corporate in character is what we may call the simple or the compound family: a man and his wife or wives and their children. In the more advanced stages of their development such families may also include the wives of married sons and their very small children. But when a man's son is old enough to perform herding duties he establishes his own separate 'household'. The new household head may maintain his father as a dependant, or his father may, along with his junior sons, maintain his own household.

Although the simple and compound family[1] rarely lives in isolation for long periods, it is, nonetheless, a viable unit, since under its head a herd is controlled and often a farm plot is cultivated. Normally a simple or compound family corresponds to what we call a 'household', but a household can best be defined as that group of individuals of both sexes who lay legitimate claim to the resources of a given herd. A household usually has a simple or compound family as its core, but there may be other individuals attached to it.

A 'herd' is defined as that group of cattle (and calves) the ownership of which is claimed by one individual (usually a male) and the calves of which are tied to a single rope (*daangol*). A household herd may include cattle in addition to those of the owner, but he exercises some control over such beasts so long as they are kept with his animals.

The dwelling place of the household we call the 'homestead'.

For his wife or wives a man builds individual shelters (*suudu*, pl. *chuudi*) the details of construction of which vary according to the season of the year, the duration of the proposed residence, and the materials at hand. Very often the shelters are simple windscreens or sun shades which may be erected, single-handed, in one

[1] In referring to the simple and compound family the Fulɓe use the term *iiyaalu*, but the vernacular term has a broad meaning. It may be applied to the members of one's household; it may be limited to a man and his wife. It may also mean all the patrilineal descendants, male and female, of a living man.

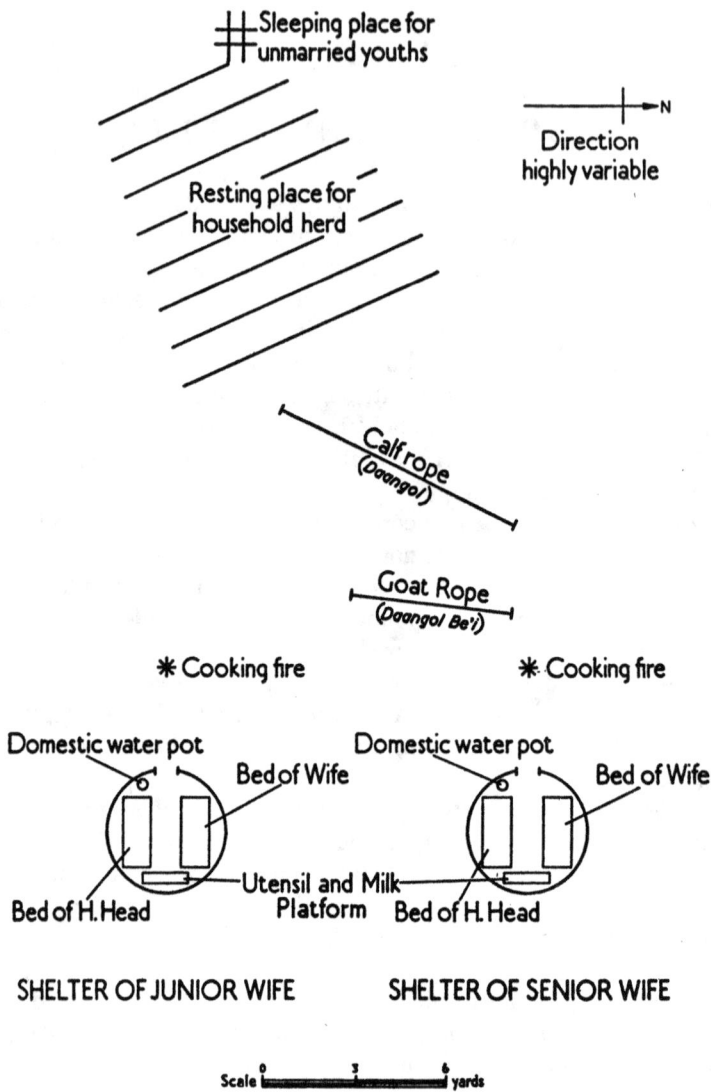

Sleeping place for unmarried youths

N
Direction highly variable

Resting place for household herd

Calf rope
(Daangol)

Goat Rope
(Daangol Be'i)

✳ Cooking fire   ✳ Cooking fire

Domestic water pot   Domestic water pot
          Bed of Wife   Bed of Wife

Bed of H. Head ——Utensil and Milk—— Bed of H. Head
                         Platform

SHELTER OF JUNIOR WIFE   SHELTER OF SENIOR WIFE

Scale ├────────┼────────┤ yards
      0   3   6

FIG. 3. Sketch-plan of homestead, polygynous family.

or two hours. The shelter is regarded as the property of the woman and if, for any reason, the wife is not present her husband will not build a shelter. The shelter serves as a sleeping place for the husband and wife and small children. It is used also as a storage place for the household utensils and food.

When possible the Fulɓe prefer to build their shelters with the entrance (*dammugal*, pl. *dammuɗe*) facing west. Since they prefer to corral their cattle to the west of their shelters they argue that at night they can easily see, without getting out of bed, if the cattle are fighting or if they have gone to pasture. They give no reason why they prefer to keep their herd to the west of the shelter except that 'it is our custom' (*ɗum al 'ada amin*). However, under certain circumstances the ideal pattern of layout is not followed. For example, when cattle are grazing swampy areas they are given the high and comparatively dry ground and the shelters are built in household clusters with the approach facing the herd. Under these conditions the orientation of the entrance is fortuitous.

The husband, especially if he is young, will spend little time in the shelter for it is regarded as the domain of his wife and he is embarrassed about being seen there in the daytime. He may sit in the shelter if it is raining and in order to have privacy when he is eating and he enters the hut more freely in the evening although even then he will prefer to be unobserved if he is newly married. During the day the husband is often in one of the nearby villages, but even if he were at home he would prefer the shade of a nearby tree to sitting in his wife's shelter.

Apart from her visits to the market the wife spends practically all her time at or near her shelter. It is here that she carries out her household tasks, grinding and cooking corn, churning, spinning in her spare time,[1] and any other chores connected with her role as wife and mother. At various times during the day, and especially before going to the market, she will spend some time trying to remove the

---

[1] Spinning is the only household craft practised by Fulɓe women. They learn how to spin as young girls and they continue the work as a spare-time craft throughout their life cycle. The spun yarn is taken to Haaɓe dyers and weavers in the villages. Money to purchase the cotton and to pay the Haaɓe craftsmen is acquired from the sale of dairy products. Women may keep the cloth for their own use or give it to their children or husband. A woman who is married and living with her husband will rarely sell yarn, but widows and unmarried women may gain an income by this means.

blemishes on her skin, plucking her eyebrows and applying kohl to her eyelids.

As a wife a woman will claim the right to admit or exclude female guests and the husband will claim the right to admit or exclude male guests. However, since the huts are small, ranging only from ten to fourteen feet at the base, and since also the adults spend most of their free time in the villages, the household shelters are not much used, either by the husband or the wife, as a place to entertain guests.

Within the hut itself there is a sleeping platform on either side of the entry way. The one on the right-hand side belongs to the husband and the one on the left-hand side belongs to the wife. Should male guests be entertained within the shelter,[1] which is generally only during inclement weather, the men sit on the husband's bed or on the ground and the women on the wife's bed or on the ground. This pattern is strictly observed in practice.

The wife is responsible for keeping the shelter reasonably clean and tidy. Her milk calabashes and household utensils should always be well scrubbed and stored in an orderly and traditional manner upon a special platform. Although they rarely express it in words to non-Fulße, husbands consider a well-kept shelter to be an index of the wife's pleasure in her marriage and an indication of her intention to try to please her husband.

The shelter is the domain of a woman acting in her role as wife and mother. In it she receives her husband almost as a guest, for a 'good' husband (by Fulße standards) spends little time in his wife's shelter since it is felt that if a woman sees too much of her husband she will fail to show him deference and respect.[2] Moreover, unless the local group is very small, a man will much prefer the society of those of his own age and sex to the companionship of

---

[1] Men prefer to entertain their friends or guests at a distance of fifty or a hundred yards from the dwellings. Usually a favourite shade tree is selected and the host tells his wife to bring the required number of mats. Having brought the mats the wife may greet the guest(s) before returning to her shelter or its precincts.

[2] This feeling is less strong when a man and his wife grow old. Seen from the point of view of the younger people, old people, since they have little 'strength' or 'intelligence', are of little value to the society and their conduct is viewed with considerable indulgence. Moreover, because the aged are always a small minority they have difficulty in finding companions of their own sex. In this context the usual rules with respect to sexual dichotomy which are so important to the younger adults are comparatively less significant to the aged and elderly.

his wife. One aspect of the attitude of men to the shelters is expressed in the phrase: '*suudu kam woni na'i yeyaaɓe*' (lit. 'the house, that is the cattle of the wives', i.e. as cattle husbandry is the work of men so household management is the work of women).

We do not discuss the formal organization of the 'camp' in this section, but at this stage it should be noted that there is considerable variation in the layout of camps which is linked with different ecological circumstances, some persistence of varying clan backgrounds, and perhaps the influence of the 'Time of War' when the larger segments of Fulɓe households lived in clan-villages.

According to an ideal expressed by some Fulɓe, when a number of households live together to form a camp the shelters should be so arranged as to indicate the seniority of the various members. Some, but not all, Fulɓe build their camps with the shelters in a line running north to south. The most senior male member (who is also the camp leader and is variously called the *jonwuro*, *'ardo*, *dikko*, and *rugga*) has the shelters of his wives in the most northerly position, the northernmost shelter being that of his most senior wife and the shelters of his junior wives ranked according to the order of their marriages. At least one clan (the Dallanko'en) hold, however, that the *jonwuro* should occupy the most southerly position. Again, two clans, the Jagadanko'en and the Bergube, whose cattle graze the most treacherous swamplands and islands of the Niger, are interested in locating well-drained sites for their homesteads—this is their overriding consideration. In general, informants feel that it is not practical today to lay out a camp according to any 'right' way since households move at irregular intervals and the location of the homestead is governed by the space available rather than by a principle of seniority.

But whatever the formal layout of the camp the individual shelters are of great importance in the sense that to children sharing a shelter, that shelter is the symbol of their being born of a common mother. In this simple shelter a strong link of affection between a mother and her children is forged, for it is here that she lavishes her affection on them. A mother and her children together fear the family head, just as they may share an antipathy to his other wife or wives. Children know that they will not receive severe discipline at the hands of their mother and she knows that she may always rely on her sons, in particular, for food, clothing, and shelter in her old age.

It should be stressed that a high degree of independence (in the broad sense of the word) is claimed by the family. The autonomy of the family influences the behaviour and the attitudes of the members who compose it. Since the family is the minimum procreative and economic unit it is within this group that we find the most intense corporate activities and interdependence. But the independence of the family has been gained at the expense of support and co-operation within a wider kinship unit. We anticipate a conclusion which is implicit in our later data when we observe that the family household as a unit is so small that when it attempts to function independently it is not without a precarious element which is most noticeable at certain stages of family development. Such a small unit is highly vulnerable to the vagaries of human and bovine fertility and mortality and to the recurrent phenomena of divorce, desertion, and the defection of its members.

The family is to be conceived as a group the individuals of which lay claim (in different ways, active and latent) to the herd or its resources. Conflicts with respect to these claims and/or the lack of their fulfilment produce centrifugal tendencies. On the other hand, the advantages of being a member of *a* family, the ecological requirements with regard to the management of a household, as well as a degree of respect for the ideal values connected with behaviour among the family members, produce centripetal tendencies. The degree of stability (or instability) which is found in any family is, to some extent, correlated with the relation between the size of the family and the size of the herd. Family heads who are most envied in the society are those who have both a sizeable family and a sizeable herd. Those who are deficient in either or both of these suffer noticeably from frustration and anxiety, for they do not enjoy a high status and they worry about the future.

In order to provide a concrete basis for further discussion we now give some quantitive data on households and herds.

9

HOUSEHOLDS AND HERDS:
A QUANTITATIVE ANALYSIS

THE quantitative information given below was collected during April and May 1953 from along a stretch of the Niger between Giri in Illo District and Besse in Besse District. The figures relate to 100 households and their herds found along this sixty-mile section of the water-course. This time and area were selected since it was necessary to have a maximum concentration of households if, working single-handed, quantitative work was to be practicable. There was such a concentration of households, since at that time (late in the dry season) the cattle were most numerous in the southerly portion of the area studied. Information was collected from all herd-owners whose cattle were grazing this sector of the islands and flood-plain of the Niger during the period of the inquiry. The figures cited are from a random sample, but the sample should have been rather larger in order to be sure that the information is typical for the Emirate as a whole. However, experience over a wider area showed no outstanding differences from the facts reported here. It will be appreciated that gathering quantitative information on pastoral peoples produces a special set of problems not the least of which is gaining their co-operation in a project which to them appears highly suspect. Then, too, the low population density of the Fulɓe and their reluctance to give numerical data put a very serious limit on the amount of field material of this sort which a research worker can gather.

In the household census those individuals whose age was estimated as over 20 years are classified as 'adults' and those younger than 20 are classified as 'minors'. There was, of course, some uncertainty (and doubtless some error) in deciding whether individuals whose actual chronological ages were probably between say 18 and 22 years should have been classed as adults or minors. However, there are means of checking these marginal cases which improves the accuracy of estimates; for example, a girl generally marries when she is 15 or 16 years old and most of her camp fellows agree as to how long she has been married. Failing this it can usually be established how long after she married she bore her first child and the ages of her children can be estimated.

Age calculation among men was easier and appeared to be more accurate than among women. It was found helpful to bring together as many men from the camp as possible and allow them to discuss their relative ages. Since relative age is an important principle of social organization, especially among men, the technique worked quite well. Thus a man, Umaru, might say, 'I am two years older than Abdu but one year younger than Musa'. From older men one gets statements such as, 'My father told me that I was born ten years after the coming of the Europeans (British Conquest 1902–3)', or, 'I was not yet weaned when the Europeans came'. Other informants link their age and the ages of their children to the year of office of a local District Head or Emir, which can be verified. Men keep track of time by remembering the number of years spent in various wet-season areas, the number of years spent with a wife or a succession of wives, when children were born, and so forth.

In general Fulɓe men especially have a good chronological sense although, of course, they do not all have the same ability and interest in this regard. For the census figures given below it can only be claimed that every effort was made to obtain as much accuracy as possible, but where age is important the results cannot, in the absence of birth registration, be absolutely precise. However, in the figures which follow significant errors are most probable in the 18 to 22 year age group. In giving the information the informants co-operated admirably and tried their very best to be accurate. When an age was not known they admitted it and when they did claim to know they generally gave convincing supporting evidence.

For 100 households the population figures are as follows:

		Percentage of total
1. Total population . . .	557	100.00
2. Total males (all ages) . .	301	54.03
3. Total females (all ages) . .	256	45.97
4. Total adult males . . .	141	25.31
5. Total adult females . .	140	25.13
6. Total adults . . .	282	50.44
7. Total male minors . .	160	28.72
8. Total female minors . .	116	20.82
9. Total minors . . .	276	49.54

The frequency distribution of household membership is as follows:

	No. of members	No. of households	Percentage of total	
1	1	0	0·00	
2	2	5	5·00 ⎫	
3	3	16	16·00 ⎪	
4	4	19	19·00 ⎪	
5	5	16	16·00 ⎬ 90%	
6	6	16	16·00 ⎪	
7	7	13	13·00 ⎪	
8	8	5	5·00 ⎭	
9	9	1	1·00	
10	10	1	1·00	
11	11	2	2·00	
12	12	2	2·00	
13	13	0	0·00	
14	14	1	1·00	
15	15	1	1·00	
16	16	1	1·00	
17	Over 16 (20)	1	1·00	
			100·00	

Except for one household with 20 members the range of household members is from 2 to 16. It is significant to note, however, that 90 per cent. of the households have a population of between 2 and 8 individuals and that 80 per cent. of the population falls between the range of 3 and 7 individuals per household. Within the sample the household population with the highest frequency is 4 of which there are 19 in the sample. The mean household population for the whole of the sample is 5·57. The significance of these figures will be discussed after figures for the herds of these households have been given.

Collecting data on the size of the herds is the most severe test of the ethnographer's ingenuity, tact, patience, and energy. In a society in which it is unthinkable to ask a man the size of his herd (or the herd of another) and is also deplorable even to look steadily at a herd, it will be appreciated that gaining this type of material is not easy. Future research workers are recommended not to approach the subject until they have a sound working knowledge of the language and enjoy the complete confidence of the people. Information on a herd was (and should be) sought only through the owner and normally in private. The technique used varied somewhat from one informant to another, but each herd-owner knew that other Fulɓe had given the same information and that the data would not be used for tax purposes or shared with other pastoralists. To count a man's cattle openly would be too great a danger to hard-won rapport. Therefore, it was decided that it would be better to persuade the informants to volunteer the information, since confidence can neither be gained nor maintained, especially among the Fulɓe, if there is a suggestion of coercion. The figures were collected in the proximity of the cattle and the fact that a count might be made acted as a check on possible deception, for they would be greatly embarrassed at giving wrong information to one whom they claimed as a friend. Whenever possible during the few daylight hours that the cattle were in the corral, and occasionally when the animals were at pasture, a reasonable number of counts were made unobtrusively and these corresponded closely with the numbers which had been volunteered. The following figures are those given by the herd-owners and checked either by a personal count or by a sight calculation. The error is probably 1–10 per cent. depending upon the size of the herd.

The total cattle population upon which the human population in the sample is dependent is 3,004. The range of the herd size for the hundred herds is as follows:

Size of herd	No. of herds	Percentage of total no. of herds
1. 10 or less	19	19·0
2. 11 to 20	20	20·0
3. 21 to 30	22	22·0
4. 31 to 40	15	15·0
5. 41 to 50	12	12·0
6. 51 to 60	5	5·0
7. 61 to 70	4	4·0
8. 71 and over (max. 90) . .	3	3·0
	100	100·0

Using these figures we arrive at a mean household herd of 30·04.

In order to make a rough comparison with the cattle population of Gwandu Emirate as a whole a random sample of figures from the 1953 tax count (July to November) was assembled. Given below is a breakdown of these herds under the same headings as above and using the same herd size units.

Sample 853 herds

Size of herd	No. of herds	Percentage of total no. of herds
1. 10 or less . . .	167	19·3
2. 11 to 20 . . .	261	30·4
3. 21 to 30 . . .	166	19·3
4. 31 to 40 . . .	98	11·4
5. 41 to 50 . . .	65	7·5
6. 51 to 60 . . .	36	4·1
7. 61 to 70 . . .	22	2·5
8. 71 and over (max. 200) .	38	4·3
	853	98·8
		Decimal error 1·2
		100·0

The mean herd using the tax-count figures is 27·9 or 2·1 below our own figures. It is of interest to note that the unit in which there is the highest percentage is the higher by 10·4. The difference may reflect a real difference in the herd sizes, but it may also mean, and this is more likely, that Fulɓe with herds which are actually larger than the 11 to 20 range reported their herds, in the official count, to be of this size. Our inference is that the Native Authority figures are probably in error on the conservative side. However, our own figures must also be regarded with some reserve since the sample is small.

We return now to give more data and to examine further the household census. Our main concern is to establish to what extent,

Sample 100 households

Unit no.	No. of males of herding age	No. of households	Percentage of total
1	1	14	14
2	2	43	43
3	3	21	21
4	4	12	12
5	5	7	7
6	6	0	0
7	7	3	3
		100	100

Total males over herding age 267
Average per household 2·67

in quantitative terms, the simple and compound family is the basic unit and also to show how certain herd-owners augment their household membership in order to meet their basic ecological requirements.

According to the ideal pattern a man will not, in normal circumstances, found his own household until he is married and has a son who has reached herding age—that is, 7 years. If this ideal were found in practice we should expect to find in the census that most households would include as a minimum two males who are at or above the herding age. The actual figures are as shown in the table at the foot of the previous page.

Now to show the degree to which these males are members of households which are basically simple and compound families we divide the households into three groups, which are:

1. Those households whose heads do not have sons of herding age.
2. Those households whose heads have minor sons who are of herding age.
3. Those households whose heads have adult sons (but who do not have patrilineal grandsons of herding age).

The figures for these classes are:

$$
\begin{array}{ll}
1.\ 39 & \text{households} \\
2.\ 50 & \text{''} \\
3.\ 11 & \text{''} \\
\hline
100 & \text{''}
\end{array}
$$

Analysis

Group 1. This group consists of simple and compound families whose children are as yet too young to undertake herding, or their children may be girls only who herd extremely rarely. The group also contains families without children (childless marriages).

Out of this group 14 household heads are without the assistance of herd-boys. The remaining 25 households received help in the following ways:

(a) Fourteen received help from younger brothers.
(b) Four hired professional herd-boys.
(c) Seven were assisted mainly by kinsmen and affines who were: 1 father-in-law, 1 wi. br., 1 mo. si. so., 1 fa. si. so., 1 fa. br. so., 2 'friends'.

Among the main reasons for the existence of the households of this group are: infertility of the spouses, infant mortality, late reproduction by (or the early death of) the household head's father, and late marriage of the present household head.

As we would expect the household heads of group 1 have the youngest average age in the sample—the head of the 39 households average 32 years of age. It is significant that in the 14 households which have but one male member (who is thus both household head and 'herd-boy') the average age is still younger, 24 years of age.

> *Group 2.* This group calls for little comment. Households of this group fulfil the ideal pattern in which the head of a simple or compound family heads the household in which the main burden of herding is carried by his minor son or sons. Out of the 50 households 9 were supplemented by junior brother(s) (married and unmarried) who did not have sons of sufficient age for them to handle an independent household.
>
> The average age of these household heads is 43 years.

> *Group 3.* This group includes those men who are approaching the age at which they will no longer act as household heads, for they are soon to be replaced by their adult sons whose children have not yet reached herding age. It is significant that at this stage of family development there are no instances in which the household head leads a fraternal family as in groups 1 and 2. The average age of the household heads is 57 years.

The above categories serve to demarcate, in a general way, the various stages through which a family passes in time. To study 'the family' in the abstract without reference to the stage of its development is as barren as to study the family without reference to the ages of the individuals who compose it. In viewing the internal structure of the family as a viable unit it is seen that the types of conflicts vary according to the stage of family development. In following this theme we now discuss the creation of the family.

10

THE CREATION OF THE FAMILY

Incentives to Marry and the Choice of Spouses

EARLIER in this report it was observed that the fondness which Fulɓe show towards cattle is linked to the fact that it is through cattle-ownership that a man may marry, beget children, and become the head of a household. It should be pointed out that Fulɓe have comparatively little concern for cattle in which they have no proprietary interest or no hope of ultimately gaining proprietary rights. Among pastoralists it is known, and is often said, that the best of all herd-boys are those youths who will become inheritors of at least a portion of the herd on the death of the present owner. The herd attendants who are the least favoured are the hirelings[1] (*biiro*, pl. *viirɓe*) who, having no hope of ultimately owning the herd, tend to be slovenly in performing their tasks as herdsmen. Hired herd-keepers often fall asleep in the pastures or visit nearby villages when they should be tending the cattle. The *viirɓe* are interested in the remuneration which they receive for herding rather than in giving careful attention to the needs of the herd. On the other hand a herd-boy who is a potential inheritor takes an interest in the herd for he knows that should the cattle remain in good condition and increase in number he will ultimately benefit.

In this analysis stress is laid upon the value which men place on becoming the head of a household, for this is a primary goal of the greatest importance. That this stress is justified will be more clearly seen when it is remembered that the household is a viable unit and also it is basically through a man's success as an efficient

---

[1] In Gwandu Emirate the 'pay' for *viirɓe* (who were always observed to be Fulɓe) is one bull a year plus food and an occasional cloth. Very occasionally, if a man favours his *biiro*, he may also provide him with marriage gifts and sufficient cattle to support a wife. While herd-owners say, with some justification, that *viirɓe* are not trustworthy, the latter say that the remuneration is not adequate, since the life is arduous and they can get better pay as labourers on the coast or by herding sheep elsewhere in the Western Sudan. The existence of a labour market outside the Emirate is a recent development and has an important influence, as will be seen, on the pattern of domestic authority.

herd-owner and household head that he gains status and prestige in his community. Indeed, after biological adulthood is reached social adulthood can be attained only if a man possesses his own herd and heads a household. It is true, of course, that as a household head a man carries heavier responsibilities in herd management than he did as a youth, but he comes to these responsibilities well qualified owing to his years of experience as a herd-boy and in sharing in discussions the pool of experience of his age-fellows. A household head also, after many years as a herd-boy, welcomes his new status when at last he has the right to delegate tasks to other members of his household. The best years of a man's life, in the Fulɓe view, are those in which he is a household head—youths look forward to the day when they will attain this position and elderly men tend to regret that they have grown old and have lost their former authority. An important aspect of father-son conflict, as we shall see, centres round a son's desire to gain social maturity as a household head. Should he press his claim a son may come into conflict with his father who, for his part, may wish to prolong the household headship which he enjoys.

In order to establish a household a man must be married, for each household requires a minimum of one woman as a working member of the unit. Among the Fulɓe marriage is regarded as the normal and desired state and all but those who are seriously disabled, mentally or physically, look forward to being married at some stage. From very early childhood children are conditioned to accept their future roles as husbands and as wives. We have already noted that young girls were observed building miniature camps and, in fantasy, acting their anticipated roles as wives and as mothers. The fantasy expression of a boy, aged about 8 years, is recorded here since it is of some interest.

Sambo, who was tending a herd of cattle in the marshlands of the Niger, sat in the shade of a tree to rest. He built two crude shelters of mud (each about one foot in diameter)—one for each of his 'wives'. He did not provide any of the traditional household utensils, nor did he concern himself with representing a 'herd'. In one shelter he placed a part of a stem of dry grass in the normal sleeping position of a household head's wife, for the piece of grass represented his first wife. Similarly he took a second piece of dry grass and broke it off to place it in the second shelter. When he attempted to place the second piece of grass in the second shelter he found that the former was too long. He did not break the stem off to make it fit within the shelter, but instead, he seized his staff—at the same time affecting much anger—and with it beat the piece of grass until it was broken into many pieces. At this point his fantasy was interrupted for he had to return to the cattle.[1]

Unfortunately the details of the family background of this boy were not obtained and even if they had been available we should not feel qualified to offer a psychological analysis of this instance of play. But attention is called to the obvious inference that the boy did show subjective interest in household headship and that he visualized himself in a superordinate role. The age of 8 years is not unusually young for a boy to express interest in household head-ship. Even boys of the age of 5 or 6 are quite aware, owing to the influence of youths and adults, that they will one day marry. Young herd-boys often say that, while their present life is very arduous and something of a drudgery, the day will come when they will control a herd and have their own sons to do the strenuous work of herding.

Because herding is both lonely and difficult most youths prefer to marry early—preferably between 20 and 25 years of age—since early marriage hastens the day of their independence and in-creased leisure. Moreover, the fear of accident or disease causes a man to give early attention to his future for which he depends on his children. According to the ideal values a man should, especially in his first marriage, marry a young bride (usually at, or just after, her puberty), but this is a point which we shall discuss further under the 'choice of sp uses'.

It is important to note that youths and men have ample oppor-tunity to obtain sexual satisfaction from Haaɓe and Fulɓe prosti-tutes in the towns and villages. But apart from the expense[2] involved, many Fulɓe are loath to patronize prostitutes since the high incidence of venereal diseases among them is well known. Both the Fulɓe and the Haaɓe have recognized herbal medicines, but many herdsmen have doubts as to their therapeutic value.[3]

---

[1] I was fortunate in having seen this case of play since children are loth to fantasy-act in the presence of adults. Sambo was so thoroughly engrossed in his play that he seemed scarcely aware of my presence, although he greeted me when I first approached. When he was beating his 'wife' he whispered invectives, the only one of which I heard was, 'you are a useless one' (*a woni banzaajo*).

[2] Prostitutes' fees vary considerably according to the age and attractiveness of the woman. The average fees come within the range of from 2 to 5 shillings.

[3] Although they were embarrassed in doing so youths and men often quietly

Another deterrent, however, to having intercourse with prostitutes is the belief held by some herdsmen that the cattle do not 'like' it if Fulɓe have relations with prostitutes. Prostitutes are regarded as 'unclean' (*laaba*) and contact with them is thought to result in a sort of pollution of the herd which causes a reduced fertility and milk yield.[1]

It is interesting to note that pre-marital sexual relations with non-prostitute Fulɓe girls do not carry a 'pollution' taboo. The main deterrent is, however, the fear, shared by sexual partners, of pre-marital pregnancy, but there is comparatively little opportunity for such pregnancy since girls marry, as we have noted, at or shortly after puberty. Generally speaking, girls and women are expected to adhere to a stricter code of sexual morality than are men and boys. However, a girl is permitted, without loss of status, to engage in sexual play in which she hopes to maintain technical virginity, for according to the ideal values a girl should go to her first husband as a virgin. It is clear, however, from the sexual case histories of youths and men that the actual behaviour of Fulɓe of both sexes does not follow a simple pattern. It will be seen that the sanctions which obtained in the past and which gave support to the ideal of pre-marital chastity (for girls in particular) have today lost much of their force. So it is that most youths and men claim to have had a few casual sexual encounters with unmarried girls. However, in guarding their local reputation a sense of responsibility for avoiding pre-marital pregnancy[2] is felt by both partners

asked me if I had medicine for gonorrhoea and syphilis. Inquiries in these cases showed that prostitutes were often the source of infection.

[1] This is an interesting example of the manner in which the Fulɓe offer a mystical explanation for the fact that those who are indolent and spendthrift (i.e. those who 'follow prostitutes') tend not to prosper.

[2] The thought of bearing an illegitimate child (*segeejo*) is regarded with horror, especially by the unfortunate mother and her immediate kin. As a rule the responsible lover will not admit his guilt unless he is prepared to marry the girl in question. If he does marry her the marriage (*kogal dole*, 'marriage of force') takes place with some haste. If the lover succeeds in fleeing to escape the consequences an effort is made to find another potential spouse, perhaps an older man, or a man of poverty. My impression is that children are seldom born out of wedlock even if the pater is not always the genitor. I found no specific cases of admitted illegitimacy (it always exists elsewhere!), although I am aware that actual cases were most likely successfully concealed. An impression of the general attitude to illegitimacy in the Moslem community is given when I mention that in Birnin Kebbi (1954) a Kaaɗo was given eighty lashes in public, on the *alkali's* orders, for calling another Kaaɗo an illegitimate child. To my knowledge this case roused little comment and no criticism from either the Fulɓe or the Haaɓe.

so that *coitus interruptus* is often practised. One further point of interest that should be noted here is that, since adults are often absent from the camp during the day, it is not uncommon for children below the age of puberty to have sexual relations. Children brought up in camps where there is comparatively little privacy, and reasoning by analogy from their observation of the herds, are very young when they first gain knowledge of the essentials of human reproduction.

Young people, while they are permitted a degree of latitude in their sexual behaviour, soon begin to give less stress to the sensuous aspect of sexual relations and become more concerned about the procreative function. It is in marriage that an individual can derive sexual satisfaction and also hope to acquire children. While young men may think it pleasant to prove their popularity among young women they know that this is but a prelude to the more serious and satisfying role of family and household headship. So it is that those who postpone marriage deliberately so that they may 'follow women' are regarded as 'wasting their strength'.[1] Such men suffer an inferiority of status, they are considered to be immature and lacking in foresight.

We shall now consider the question of the choice of spouse. It should be noted at the outset that the qualities sought in a potential spouse are by no means uniform. This lack of uniformity is, to some extent, linked with the wider process of social change in the society, as well as being due to personal differences and to the age of the individual in question.

In keeping with the fact that young men tend to stress the sexual aspects of their relations with women, it is not surprising that young suitors tend to favour girls who are attractive by the standards of the society: a light skin, a long narrow nose, a long neck, long thick hair kept in attractive plaits and a firm, well-developed bosom. However, as a man grows older, though he may still seek a wife who is attractive, he tends to consider a wider range of factors. One of the most important of these is her 'character' (*gikku*). A woman with a good *gikku* should show obedience to her

---

[1] In the vernacular '*ɓe ndufai sembe maɓɓe*', 'they spill their strength'. This alludes to the wastage of seminal fluid which is considered to have its greatest potency when a man is young; it also refers to the cumulative influence of regular copulation which is thought to lead to the progressive weakening of a man and the strengthening of his sexual partner. To support their argument on the latter point Fulɓe hold that women live longer than men.

husband, respect his senior kin and be amiable to his friends. She should, above all, be faithful to him even though she cannot claim exclusive rights to his sexual favours. She should, as a sexual partner, give him free access except, of course, during periods of recognized prohibition[1] and during times of illness. In the act of sexual intercourse she should remain passive, for such is the mark of a woman who is modest and of good character—the overt expression of pleasure is behaviour typical of a prostitute. In her personal hygiene a woman should conscientiously perform the ablutions enjoined by Islam and she should keep herself as clean as the local conditions allow. A good wife should always be cheerful and kindly. A further and important qualification is that a wife should be a frugal manager of her household. She is expected to cook clean, ample, and tasty food on what are often meagre resources. In brief a woman who has good *gikku* should have all those traits of personality and character which are embodied in Fulɓe values. Only the most important of these have been noted above.

In passing value judgements on modern women, Fulɓe men speak of their lack of morality in comparison with the past when, living in larger local kin groups and being less active in the household economy, because of slaves, their behaviour could be more strictly controlled by men.[2] As an important general point it should be stated that men have little confidence in the faithfulness of women, who, given an opportunity, will, it is thought, freely have illicit love affairs. In this connexion a typical remark is: '*heɓugo debbo sada amma heɓugo debbo mo gikku i chaddum*' ('to obtain (marry) a woman is not difficult, but to obtain a woman of good character is not easy').

It is flattering for a man to have a wife who is attractive and who is known to have a good character, for it reflects on his popularity since it is likely that such a woman has had many suitors. But in

---

[1] These are: during menstruation and a variable period before and after child-birth. The idea of having sexual relations during menstruation is as unthinkable to a woman as it is distasteful to a man. Men and women who ignore the prohibition are believed to risk contracting leprosy, although not all lepers are thought to suffer the disease because of this irregularity.

[2] In the past, it is said, the work of a housewife was confined to supervising the labour of female slaves. In these circumstances Fulɓe women were confined to their respective households and there was little opportunity for them to meet potential lovers. Today, on the other hand, since women market dairy products their movements are not easily observed by their husbands and there is ample opportunity for clandestine affairs.

seeking out a future wife a suitor may well overlook the absence of otherwise desirable traits if the woman in question is likely to bring cattle to his homestead.[1] This is because more prestige is derived from having a herd of respectable size than from being married to a woman who possesses the acknowledged virtues. The desire to gain wealth through marriage is best expressed in the vernacular phrase: 'if one finds a woman with cattle, whether a Kaaɗo or a leper, marry her' (*kul neɗɗo na tawai debbo mo na'i, 'in o Kaaɗo, 'in o kuturuujo, sei howa*). In point of fact no specific instances were recorded in which a Pullo married either a Kaaɗo or a leper in order to gain wealth (no instances were recorded in which Haaɓe women owned cattle in significant numbers), but since such a marriage would normally be regarded with revulsion the statement gives, by its exaggeration, an indication of the attitude towards marrying in such a manner as to acquire cattle.

Even though men may desire to marry a woman with cattle, the ownership of these animals by women is regarded as anomalous and contrary to Fulɓe tradition. One view of herdsmen on this point is given in the idiomatic expression: '*njaudi debbo, gauri faandu, jangde Kaaɗo, olco teeto*' ('a woman with wealth (cattle), a little corn in a bottle gourd and a Kaaɗo with learning (Moslem) all make a lot of noise').[2] It should be noted that just as men consider it unusual for a woman to own cattle they also feel that if they marry such a woman they may expect atypical behaviour from her. Men, therefore, expect (and often find) that a woman who has many cattle will be disobedient and fail to show respect since she, unlike women without cattle, will always be able to find a husband —even after she has passed her menopause. Here again a typical statement sums up the view held by men on this point: '*kul deeka omo heewi risku nden gorko omo jogi sauru banza*' ('if a wife has much

---

[1] Women can own cattle in two ways: by inheritance (see sub-section below on inheritance, p. 137) and through an institutionalized gift of a heifer (*chuchuki*) given by the father. However, since brothers have a prior claim to household cattle, only a small minority of women own cattle in significant numbers. During her lifetime a woman gives her cattle to her sons as they establish their separate households and on her death, if any cattle remain, they are inherited by her sons as though she was their father.

[2] This is a succinct reference to the view that women are no more qualified (and accustomed) to own cattle than Haaɓe are to have knowledge in Islam. In contrast, Fulɓe men are by tradition both learned in Islam and owners of cattle and accordingly they carry these burdens modestly.

wealth then her husband carries his staff in vain'—that is, he cannot use his staff to discipline his wife).

In summing up the qualities which are sought in a potential wife we may say that possibly no two suitors have identical ideals. Generally speaking, however, a man attempts to choose a wife with whom he feels that he will best meet the problems of his future married life. Some men feel a strong desire to marry a woman with wealth (in cattle) for, apart from the prestige they hope to gain in having a larger herd before their homestead, they hope to depend less on their own herds alone for economic security. Again, some men stress the importance of a wife being trustworthy and of good character, for the viability of monogamous households, in particular, is always threatened if the housewife is not dependable. Indeed, informants have often expressed the view, as we shall see, that it is best to maintain a polygynous household because if one wife leaves, the household will continue to be self-sufficient. Still other men place a high value on a woman who is agreeable and cheerful, since with such a wife the life at the homestead is pleasant. Finally, in the choice of a wife, her character is important not only for the reasons mentioned above but also because, in the Fulɓe view, children tend to inherit their characters from their mother: '*endu ɓuri ɓadaago gabaare*' ('the bosom is closer (to the child, in the genetic sense) than is the chest' (of the genitor)). A child resembles its mother in character because it was within the womb during the period of gestation and was suckled for a period of two years. If a man wishes to beget children who are obedient and trustworthy then he should marry a woman who has these traits.

We turn now to a discussion of the choice of a spouse as seen from the points of view of a potential bride and her parents.

Girls and women are not compelled to marry against their will, although they may be strongly influenced by their parents, in particular by the mother. Parents attempt to persuade a daughter to marry a given man, but they rarely try to force their choice on her since they know that she will not stay with a man whom she dislikes even if they are successful in marrying her against her will. It was the unanimous opinion of a series of informants of both sexes that the pattern of revolt against parental authority on the part of marriageable daughters is a post-Protectorate phenomenon. During the 'Time of War', it is said, after a spouse was chosen for a girl by her parents, the girl was asked if she agreed to the choice. According to the same informants, the girl would almost invariably agree to the marriage, since she faced the concerted opinion of a comparatively large group of kin of the parental generation and she knew that their decision had already been made. Today, however, a girl is responsible to her parents alone and there are various ways in which she can escape a marriage which is repugnant to her. A girl who is not pleased with the suitor chosen by her parents may bring shame on her family by leaving home and becoming a prostitute, for unlike girls in the past, the outside world holds few terrors for a modern milkmaid. Another girl in similar circumstances may elope (*kogal siiri*, 'secret marriage') with a suitor whom she favours. These two sanctions—the threat to become a prostitute and to marry secretly—are said to have been non-existent in the past. While this view held by the informants is probably not strictly accurate there is ample evidence to confirm our view that the threat of the use of these sanctions, or their actual application, has increased in recent years. But there is another sanction which a girl may use against her parents, which, according to our information, was used during the 'Time of War'. This was suicide, which some informants say was more frequent in the past than it is today. Since suicide is such a serious action, the threat of committing it is itself an important sanction. In order to show how the threat of suicide may come into play we cite an example from our field notes.

Satu was obliged, owing to pressure from her father, to marry a man whom she did not favour. It is doubtful if the marriage would have taken place if Satu's mother had been alive since it is likely that she would have supported the objection of her daughter. However, although Satu would have been within her rights in refusing to marry the man, in deference to her father she married and went to live at the homestead of her suitor. About a year after her marriage Satu returned to the homestead of her father and said that she could no longer live with her husband. Some days later the husband came to the homestead of Satu's father and said that he wanted his wife to return to him. Satu refused to return and added that, if she were forced to go back, she would end her life by throwing herself into a well. Her father did not believe her so, along with his son-in-law, he bound Satu in ropes and placed her in a canoe to take her back to her husband's homestead.

On the return voyage, despite the fact that she was bound, Satu was able to jump overboard and was rescued by her father and her husband. But after this incident her father said that Satu would indeed commit suicide if she was forced to return to her husband. She was taken back to the homestead of her father and shortly afterwards obtained a formal divorce in the *alkali's* court.

A few days after her divorce Satu married a suitor of her own choice whom she had known and 'desired' before her first marriage.

It is possible that when the Fulɓe lay such stress on their tendency to commit suicide they are making another of their many attempts to distinguish themselves from the Haaɓe for whom they have a hearty contempt. Fulɓe accept the Moslem doctrine that suicide is a sin against God (*laifi i Allah*) and that one who commits the offence will be cast into Hell. Nevertheless, they regard their disposition to suicide almost as a virtue since it is an expression of extreme grief and a sense of injury as well as an act which requires much courage. Fulɓe say that the Haaɓe are not similarly disposed, since they are insensitive to shame and certainly lack the fortitude required of one who would take his own life.

In modern Fulɓe society, if a girl has means by which she can escape the oppressive authority of her parents, there are also advantages in her remaining on good terms with them, which means complying with their wishes. Particularly in the early years of her marriage a girl relies on the support of her parents should there be a crisis in her marriage. If there is a divorce (an event of frequent occurrence see p. 145) she will spend the interval until her next marriage with her parents.[1] A further point is that a girl may wish to remain in favour with her father in particular for, if he has sufficient cattle and is pleased with his daughter, he may give her several cows to take to her husband's homestead after she has borne her first child. In point of fact less than a third of the women marrying today receive such cattle (*chogitaaɗi*) from their fathers, but women are very eager to obtain their own cattle since they know that as a rule women who own cattle receive better treatment from their husbands.

In general we may say that some daughters accept with little question the decisions made on their behalf by their parents. Other daughters let it be known that on certain issues they intend, by the means noted above, to escape parental authority if it is too harsh. Between these extremes are those parents and daughters who, in the interest of harmonious relations within the family,

[1] In this report I do not give figures on the frequency of divorce and desertion in Fulɓe marriage. I hope to write a paper on this subject in due course.

weigh and discuss their differences and through compromise arrive at decisions which are agreeable to both parties.

Once a girl has reached the age of puberty her parents are interested in marrying her as soon as possible, for today parents have difficulty in exercising their authority over daughters and there is some fear of pre-marital pregnancy. Then too it is realized that the reproductive cycle of a woman is shorter than that of a man so that women should, in Fulɓe theory, marry younger than men. Moreover, the marriage of a daughter need not be delayed owing to the poverty of her natal household (as is the case with men) since the main burden of the marriage gifts is borne by the potential groom and/or his father[1] (see below, 'Marriage Gifts', pp. 84 ff.).

The fact that women marry very young is relevant to a discussion on the choice of a husband because the responsibility felt by a parent for a child is, to some extent, related to the age of the child.

In some degree parents today, in choosing a spouse for their daughter, have adjusted their attitudes to the modern social and ecological conditions of the community. Informants say that in the past, when 'most' people were betrothed to and married their cousins,[2] there was much solidarity (*sumpo*) between siblings of both sexes because of the marriage of their children, and between husband and wife there was also affection because of the kinship of their parents. It is stated further that since the parents of both spouses lived in the same village they intervened in the disputes between spouses to try to preserve the conjugal and jural bonds of the marriage. Disputes between spouses were then considered to be very serious since it was believed that if they were allowed to develop they might cause a cleavage within the larger kin-group.

Informants hold that marriage has always been a relationship of potential conflict since the 'plan' (*dabare*, also outlook, and stratagem) of a man differs from that of a woman. If one marries a kinsman it is felt that the likelihood of conflict is less since the affection and disposition to co-operate, which obtain among kinsmen (and clansmen), should override the latent conflict. There is ample evidence that during the 'Time of War' an important function of

---

[1] The practice of giving cattle (*chogitaadi*) to a married daughter is not obligatory. The gift tends to be given only by those fathers who can afford it and giving the gift may be regarded in part as a bid for prestige.

[2] The only cousin with whom marriage was not (and is not) favoured was the matrilateral parallel cousin (*ɓiddo inna'en*).

marriage was to give expression to the ideal values implied in the obligations of kinship.[1] Kinsmen and clansmen who as parents felt special bonds of affection for each other proclaimed their affection by the betrothal of their children and thereby expressed a desire to give permanence to the happy relationship. Since the tie between siblings was strong a man preferred to betroth his son or daughter to a child of his brother or his sister. A woman preferred her son or daughter to marry her brother's child. If a potential spouse did not have a marriageable cousin, then a more remote kinsman or clansman would be chosen.

Today most informants say that it is good to marry one's cousin, although there is no agreed opinion as to which category of cousins should marry. The exception to the preference of a cousin is the mother's sister's child, marriage with whom is regarded with disfavour and such marriages are rarely found in practice.

In this connexion the progressive dispersal of the clan during the present century is relevant, since it has an important bearing on the attitudes and actions of parents when they approve of a suitor as a husband for their daughter. Mention has been made above of the earlier solidarity of the clan, in general, and of the sibling group in particular. That solidarity was a function of the enforced co-residence of a comparatively large group. In contrast, today the viability of households and their freedom of independent movement strongly militate against the formation of cohesive permanent groupings. It is the mobility of households which is most clearly linked with the reduction in strength of the ties of kinship and clanship, for these bonds cannot survive spatial separation indefinitely. Not only is it difficult technically to arrange endogamous marriages when the clan is dispersed through the community but also the motive for such marriages has weakened. Thus in specific marriage histories it is seen that parents may accept as a husband for their daughter a man whom they have known for some time and with whose circumstances and character they are familiar, rather than a kinsman or a clansman who is a comparative stranger.

[1] The usual distinction made by anthropologists between kinsmen and clansmen is not found in Fulfulde. Kinsmen and clansmen alike are *ɓiɓɓe lenyol* ('children of the clan'). When, however, kinship is known the appropriate referent is used rather than the more general term for clansman, *bandirao*. Actually, today, the term *bandirao* may be extended to include all Fulɓe with whom a man comes into contact. But this is a recent departure from the traditional usage.

It is an index of the viability of households and their independence of outlook that today marriage is predominantly the concern of the two family households of which the potential spouses are members.

It is true that the incidence of cousin marriage remains relatively high[1] although it is much lower, Fulɓe believe, than in the past. But we are here viewing attitudes and actions from the point of view of their adaptation to the modern social and ecological reality and it is the present trends which are of the most interest to us.

On her marriage a girl usually lives in virilocal residence, but occasionally she may live in neolocal residence. Parents realize that under present conditions they may be separated from their daughter by a distance which may preclude frequent visits. She may visit the same market as her parents only seasonally, or she may be more or less permanently separated from them. It is not always possible, therefore, for a daughter to refer her day to day marital problems to her mother as she did in the 'Time of War'. For this reason parents try to learn something of the character of the suitor for they are concerned that their daughter should not suffer abuse from him or from his kin. It is true that a wife who feels that she has a legitimate complaint against her husband may report to the *alkali*—one of whom is generally within a day's walking distance of any camp—but this is usually done only if her parents live far away.

[1] I give here a quantitative analysis of the number of cousin marriages (real and classificatory) recorded in a random sample of the first marriages of 200 living men of all ages. I do not give a refined statistical analysis of these cases showing age distribution and so forth, since I plan to do this in a later paper in which the wider implications of the figures will be indicated. I have shown only first marriages because it is in these unions that the obligation to marry cousins is the strongest. Since the sample includes men of all ages who have had marital experience the figures include unions which were completed as early as the beginning of the present century. The incidence of cousin marriages would be less if we considered only present-day marriages.

						% real	% class.
1. First marriages to:	Mo. Br. Da.	.		.	.	13·0	4·5
2. ,,	,,	,,	Fa. Br. Da.	.	.	.	12·0	3·0
3. ,,	,,	,,	Fa. Si. Da.	.	.	.	10·0	2·5
4. ,,	,,	,,	Mo. Si. Da.	.	.	.	0·5	2·0
Total percentage cousin marriages				.	.	35·5	12·0

Total percentage cousin marriages (real and classificatory) 47·5

Parents are very much concerned that a future son-in-law should have the resources with which to support a wife and should be industrious (*tiďďuďo*) and efficient as a cattle husbandman. Thus a youth once reported to the observer that his parents-in-law allowed him to marry their daughter because they had known him for some time and, although he was neither a kinsman nor a clansman, they recognized him as a hard worker and a skilled herdsman. The informant married the girl even though she had a number of suitors living nearby who as kinsmen and clansmen were otherwise preferable. It is generally believed that a man who is devoted to his cattle is a 'good' Pullo and as such he should make an agreeable husband. With such a man a woman should be content, for she will receive 'correct' treatment, nice clothing, and, because of adequate nourishment, she should bear many healthy children—the foundation upon which any marriage rests.

In general parents wish a daughter to marry within the pastoral community a man who will attend to her material needs and within limits treat her kindly. A household head prefers the resources of his corral to be used to support his wife or wives and small children rather than his mature daughters or sisters, for it is only as a wife that a woman completely fulfils both her economic and her reproductive functions. A woman belongs in the household of her husband; if she lives in the household of either her father or her brother she is an unnecessary drain on the resources of these households. Congruently, marriages of long duration are favoured as an ideal, for divorce and desertion are not only unpleasant when they occur, but are also disruptive of the subsistence of the households concerned. This is so because, as we have seen, the viable family household is a small unit. So the head of a monogamous household is in a difficult position should his wife leave him; he must depend either on his mother, or perhaps a brother's wife, for prepared food until he can arrange another marriage or persuade his wife to return. Moreover, if a wife returns to the household of her father or her brother—especially during the dry season when food is in short supply—she will put strain on their domestic economy. Accordingly, when parents agree to a suitor's marrying their daughter it is with the hope that the marriage will last so that they will be free of responsibility for her future support.

Since there is little economic co-operation between households the best security against privation is an adequate herd. It is said that, in the 'Time of War', if a man was poor his kinsmen and clansmen would lend him slaves or cattle until he could restore his prosperity. Thus the relative wealth of a suitor was not so important as it is today when each household is self-supporting.

However, today when parents allow or persuade their daughter to marry a relatively wealthy man it is not with a view to securing their own future. It is on their sons that parents rely for their subsistence when they grow old. It was found, for example, that in the 100 sample households referred to above only in one instance did a man live with, and gain his support from, his married daughter in her husband's home.[1] In the same sample there were no instances of a woman living with her daughter in the household of her son-in-law.

From the foregoing we can see that when parents approve of a given suitor they do so on the basis of their experience and they take into account certain practical considerations. On the other hand, young potential brides favour the so-called *kogal yidde* (marriage of 'affection' or 'love') in which they profess a strong liking for their potential spouse. They may be attracted by the man's personality, his sense of humour, his attractiveness, and so forth, and they tend to give less consideration to the qualities which their parents would seek in a suitor were they arranging the marriage.

There are certain other vernacular terms the meaning of which should be noted. The term *piɓol* (from the infinitive *fiɓugo*, 'to tie') refers to a marriage which was the culmination of a child betrothal. *Kogal saarooji*[2] may be used as a synonym for *piɓol*, but more often it is used to specify a marriage in which the parents of the spouses, although taking the initiative in arranging the marriage of their children, did not do so until the affianced had both reached puberty. Another type of marriage is the *kogal daɓɓol* (from the infinitive *daɓɓugo*, 'to seek, to go and get') in which the potential groom himself chooses the person whom he wishes to marry. After his first marriage (and today often in the first marriage) a man generally marries in *kogal daɓɓol*. Especially when both spouses are young

---

[1] The anomaly of this situation is seen in the inversion of the orthodox social usages. That is, normally the son-in-law would always pay much deference and respect to his father-in-law. In this case, however, since the father-in-law owned no cattle he served as herd-attendant for his son-in-law to compensate the latter for his support.

[2] *Saarooji* is the vernacular term for 'parents'.

this type of marriage is usually also a *kogal yidde*, since the spouses have themselves decided to marry after becoming acquainted at evening meetings in the camps or in Haaɓe villages. *Piɓol* and *kogal saarooji* are becoming less frequent today.

Although we have given considerable space to the discussion of the choice of spouses the information which we have given has been greatly over-simplified. This is necessary since the society is undergoing a marked change and, as in other societies, the process does not affect all individuals equally—even those of the same age and sex who are living within the same community and appear superficially to have had the same background of experience. Individual variations in temperament and outlook are always present and, indeed, no one could be more aware of this than the Fulɓe themselves, who speak of human personalities as being like the fingers of one's hand—no two are alike.

Because of culture lag and individual variation we do not find a uniform pattern of values and attitudes on the question of the choice of spouses. However, one clearly discernible trend is that, just as the household enjoys independence in the economic sense, so also it claims autonomy in respect of decisions to marry the members which compose it. For example, it is not uncommon in these days for a man to arrange the marriage of his children without first consulting either his parents or his siblings. Indeed, marriage case histories recorded show instances in which young men herding cattle away from their close kin have married for the first time entirely on their own initiative. The cumulative effect of these and similar actions is the gradual and piecemeal rejection of some of the traditional values and attitudes and their replacement by those which are more congruent with the modern social structure.

Having discussed the qualifications which are sought in a potential spouse, by the parents, on the one hand, and by the future spouses on the other we shall now consider marriage gifts from two broad aspects: firstly, the circumstances in which marriage gifts may vary in economic value, and secondly, the actual range in value of those gifts.

11

ECONOMIC ASPECTS OF MARRIAGE GIFTS

AMONG informants of both sexes there was general agreement that the value of marriage gifts has increased in recent years. In seeking an explanation for the phenomenon they say that the increase is due to the break-down of clan endogamous marriages. That is, in modern marriage the possibility of material advantages is stressed, whereas formerly any union, as we have seen, was an attempt to strengthen close ties which existed between the parents of the spouses. In the latter context, it is said, giving of gifts was incidental, for the 'pleasure' (*belɗum*) of strengthening an existing bond between parents was primary.

Our own view is that marriage gifts have increased also because in modern marriage there is a pronounced competitive aspect. Nubile girls, divorced or widowed women do not remain unmarried for long, since news of their status travels quickly and suitors will soon, whether or not they are kinsmen or clansmen, make offers of marriage. For this reason even a suitor who is favoured by a potential bride (and/or her parents) must offer generous gifts or be embarrassed by another suitor whose gifts are more attractive.

But if generous gifts, by Fulɓe standards, are required in order to get married, a man's ability adequately to support his wife is an important factor in his ability to maintain the union. If a man is asked why he does not take another wife he replies that he cannot afford to support another wife—he does not say that he cannot afford the required gifts. An axiom current among men is that women are less tolerant of hunger and general deprivation than are men.

While marriage gifts in general have increased in value in recent years, equally significant is the fact that there is some range in the value of the gifts which are transferred in individual marriages. As a general statement which needs little qualification we may say that the value of marriage gifts is highest in unions with young women and lowest in marriages with older (from the point of view of marriage) women. However, just as there is some range in the expense of marrying 'young' women so also there is variation in the cost of marrying 'old' women. The interaction of the factors affecting the cost of getting married are extremely complex, but the basic principles are comparatively simple and it is with these that we are concerned.

Broadly speaking the cost of marrying any woman is a direct function of what might be called her marriage value. Since, in the Fulɓe view, the most important purpose in marriage is the procreation of children, the higher marriage value of young women is directly linked to the fact that their entire reproductive cycle lies before them and thus, all other factors being equal, they are likely to bear the most children. The presence or absence of those qualifications noted above, which are sought in women, affects to some extent a suitor's marriage expenses regardless of the age of a potential wife.

The bridegroom's expenses are greater when the bride has not been married before than they would be if he were marrying a woman who had been married previously, if only because in the first instance a bull must be provided for ceremonial killing. It is a matter of pride that the bull[1] should be young (usually 2 to 3 years) and in good condition. It may either be taken from the groom's own herd (or that of his father) or purchased in the market. Such animals had a value of from £7 to £12 in 1954.

The *kirsil* of a girl's first marriage is expensive but the right of a previously unmarried youth to marry a girl without marital experience is not questioned. One who in his first marriage did not marry a virgin or putative virgin may be gibed at by his age-fellows who may say, 'you have never enjoyed the pleasure of intercourse with a virgin'. The implication being that he is without 'popularity'[2] (*togu*) or his family could not afford to part with a bull.

---

[1] Called *kirsil*, from the root *hirsuugo*, 'to kill'; the suffix *il* is the diminutive form of the noun.

[2] Lack of popularity is very closely linked with poverty. Fulɓe say that wealth and popularity 'are the same thing'. Even among children popularity rating is done very largely on the basis of the wealth of their respective parents. In this general connexion I should like to mention a significant field incident. One day an attractive girl of about 12 years of age came to me in tears and said that she had spent the afternoon crying and she felt so upset that she would like to throw herself into a well. Some new beads had come into the local market, but she did not have a shilling to buy a pair. Her girl 'friends' had taunted her and said, 'you must come from "useless" parents who cannot even afford a shilling so that you can have nice beads'. I gave her a shilling—after a firm promise that she would not tell anyone (so that I would not become thought of as a local emergency

A smaller proportion of men in unions subsequent to their first may also marry girls who are marrying for the first time. But there is a feeling that in her first marriage a girl should marry a partner who is without previous marital experience. However, when old men do marry the previously unwed it is, among other things, with a view to showing that they are still attractive to women and that they can afford the additional costs of a first marriage.

An important general point which should be stressed here is that, as a rule, when a man is marrying for the first time (being still a dependant in the household of his father) not only does his father usually give a bull, but in other respects also his marriage is considerably more expensive than, for example, a later marriage of his father's. Another important point is that, from the point of view of a father with a number of sons, the giving of a bull for each son can amount to a considerable drain on the household herd. However, by the same token, a large number of sons is a great asset since they are likely to tend the family herd efficiently (and hence the herd may have a higher reproductive rate) and the surplus labour of dependent sons will be used in farming.

The killing of the bull is done by Haaɓe professional butchers from a nearby village. At the same time the first verse of the Koran (*fatiya*) is read—usually by a Kaaɗo *mallam* (H. F. *modiibo*)—and after this point the marriage is legally recognized. The *mallam* also prays for good health, children and wealth for the spouses. The prayer is said in Arabic and few Fulɓe can understand it. Regardless of the fortunes of the marriage, it is only on the grounds of non-consummation that the groom or his father can claim compensation for the *kirsil*. Informants are rarely explicit as to the social function of the slaughter but it is quite certain that the bull is held to be provided for the groom's privilege of defloration. The fact that a proportion of modern girls do not go to their first husbands as virgins does not seem to affect the issue.

If the bride were to die after the bull had been killed but before consummation her death would be regarded as the 'work of God' and no groom would be so niggardly as to demand compensation. Despite careful inquiries no case was recorded in which compensation in cash or kind was claimed or paid for a slaughtered *kirsil*.

According to Maliki Law, only one gift, known as *sadaaki* (H.

fund!)—and while she thanked me profusely she was so delighted that she almost lost her coherence. She too could have new beads.

and F.; Ar. *sadaq*) is required to ensure that the contract of marriage is legally binding. But no Pullo questioned was aware of this point, for they believe that other gifts, to be mentioned presently, are also required. Before reading the *fatiya* the *mallam* asks three witnesses if the *sadaaki* has been given. If it has not he will not perform the ceremony.

The value of the *sadaaki* tends to vary according to whether the future wife has previously been married and also according to her age and her general marriage value. To a girl who has not previously been married her suitor (or his representative) will give a heifer as *sadaaki*.[1] If a man's future bride was formerly married, but is still young and has a lot of suitors, he may still give her a heifer.

The heifer and its future offspring remain the property of the wife so long as conjugal and jural relations with her husband remain intact. In theory, but not always in practice, the property remains hers even in the case of divorce, provided it is established that the marriage was not terminated on account of 'wrong' conduct on her part. If, on the other hand, a wife deserts her husband, or if she clearly conducts herself so as to provoke her husband to repudiate her, then she automatically forfeits her claim to the *sadaaki*. This is the view taken by the Native Authority courts with respect to *sadaaki* settlement in divorce and desertion cases. But only a fraction of Fulɓe divorce cases reach the courts. In out of court settlements a husband will seldom permit *sadaaki*-born cattle to leave his herd. A woman is a legal minor and, without the local support of her kin, is not in a strong position to defend her rights.

It should be noted that, while a man may give his wife a heifer in *sadaaki*, it is only rarely that the gift involves an economic sacrifice, since the heifer, along with its future offspring, remains in his herd. And, as we have seen, even in the case of divorce or desertion it is unlikely that he will part with any animals. If, however, after his formal repudiation of his wife, a man permits *sadaaki* to be removed from his herd, this is a gesture made in order to absolve himself of guilt in the marital conflict and to embarrass his former wife and affines by making them appear greedy in accepting the animals.

---

[1] Unlike the *kirsil* described above a heifer as *sadaaki* is not referred to by a special term. It is called *bi nagge* (lit. 'the offspring of a cow') which is the general term for a heifer regardless of the context.

If a man marries a woman in her late twenties or older, the *sadaaki* is usually a cash gift. The range is from about 5s. to a few pounds. Women who are on the verge of, or past the menopause will, of course receive the lower amount. When *sadaaki* is paid in cash, even if the marriage ends before consummation, it is unlikely that the giver will ask for the return of this gift, or accept it if offered to him. Acceptance of the refund of *sadaaki* in cash is regarded by some as niggardly and a husband may (although he does not always) refuse it, since he feels that by accepting it he may lose popularity and therefore have difficulty in marrying in the future. A number of informants, when asked why they did not accept the return of *sadaaki* in cash, answered simply, '*gam jaango*' (lit. 'because of tomorrow').

The marriage gift that is most variable in value is the *tooshi*,[1] which is almost always a cash gift and is given in all marriages except the *kogal sadaka*[2] ('marriage of alms'). The maximum is about £12, but the mean is in the range of from £2 to £7.

In his first marriage *tooshi* is provided by the man's father. When a man is taking a second or subsequent wife he provides the gift himself, although, as at his first marriage, he may receive a nominal contribution from siblings and from his matrilateral and patrilateral grandparents, but this is the exception rather than the rule. Today the seasonal and permanent dispersal of kin militates against a kin-group contributing to and receiving shares of marriage gifts. This is another aspect of modern household independence.

Tooshi is received by the parents of the bride and is used largely, if not entirely, to buy new clothing for her and to purchase her household and milk utensils. If the *tooshi* is adequate, a small

---

[1] This term is probably of Hausa origin. Major R. C. Abraham (*Dictionary of the Hausa Language*, 1949) defines the term as a 'bribe'—a 'present to win a person over'. Dr. M. G. Smith (*The Economy of Hausa Communities of Zaria*, 1955, p. 59) considers *tooshi* to be a gift to secure favour but not a bribe for a specific act. In my experience the Fulɓe use the word in the context of marriage, as described above, and also speak of *toshin sallah*, the gifts given by, or on behalf of a betrothed boy (at the time of Ramadan) to his betrothed or her guardian.

[2] In the total marriage experience of about 300 men I recall but one case of *kogal sadaka*. It is a matter of Fulɓe pride to make some marriage payment, however slight. As Dr. M. G. Smith says (ibid., p. 55), *kogal sadaka* (H. *auren sadaka*) is a form of almsgiving and it applies to *mallams*. There are few cattle-owning Fulɓe *mallams*, although it is said that there were many more during the 'Time of War'; pastoral youths have little time and often little inclination to go to Koranic schools.

portion may be given to those individuals who might have contributed were the forthcoming marriage that of a son rather than a daughter. If the *tooshi* is large the bride's mother may spend some of it on cloth for her own use.

According to several elderly women who claim to have been married in the last decade of the nineteenth century, there has been an important change in the *tooshi* during the present century. One woman, for example, who claims to be 78 years old (1954), said that at the time of her marriage (*circa* 1895) the *tooshi* was standardized at one cowrie shell—and that was for a first marriage. If this is so then the gift could have had only a token value since, by modern purchasing power, a cowrie shell was then worth about 100th of a penny. If the *tooshi* was formerly a cowrie shell this may have been a local variation, or it may have been a temporary voluntary reduction while the herdsmen recouped themselves for their losses in the great rinderpest epidemic (1887–91).[1] Detailed information indicates that, generally speaking, there has been a gradual increase in *tooshi* in the past fifty years or so, but this increase has not been greatly out of keeping with the increase in the cost of living for the same period.

There are a limited number of factors which influence the amount of *tooshi* paid in any marriage. The very highest *tooshi* payments were made, in our sample, by youths and young men who, having accumulated savings (usually by herding sheep in Bornu), put on a conspicuous display of wealth[2] and, by offering *tooshi* payment in excess of the local standard, hoped to, and did in fact, compete favourably with other suitors.

Tooshi payment may also be high when a suitor, enamoured of a woman who is already married, is obliged to provide a second *tooshi* since he must replace the same gift paid by the first husband should he, on divorce, demand its return.

Finally, we have already noted that certain marriageable girls in any community are more popular than others and for such girls there is much competition. The parents of a popular girl may begin marriage arrangements for their daughter by accepting the *tooshi* of a likely suitor. Unless, for any reason, they have a strong

[1] See above, pp. 16, 49.

[2] During the wet season of 1954 I met a man of about 20 years of age who was marrying two young women within a week. He was newly returned from Bornu and was using his own money. He would not be able to marry in such quick succession if he were still dependent on his father.

preference for him they may accept a higher *tooshi* from a second suitor and refund the gift of the former. They will then make some excuse to the first suitor for their decision not to proceed with the marriage plans. If a girl has five or more suitors obviously the suitor who finally marries her must make a large payment.

In the first marriage of a daughter the *tooshi* may be accepted some months before the reading of the *fatiya*. From the point of view of the parents of the future bride this has some advantages. The fact that they have accepted *tooshi* makes it known to other men that their daughter is to marry and other suitors who may be more desirable may come forward. Parents may also inquire further into the background of a suitor with a view to learning if he is suitable for their daughter. A few case histories showed that *tooshi* had been returned to a suitor because a more desirable man came forward: this may in fact have happened more often than was reported to the observer. Men like to think that they are irresistible and to have the money returned is an affront to their pride. Other men reported that when the parents of their proposed bride offered to return the money they refused it.

When a man is marrying a woman who is older and not so much sought after, he may make a single payment of cash to cover both the *sadaaki* and the *tooshi* and the marriage ceremony may take place within but a few days. A man who is already established as a household head may be in urgent need of a wife and not prepared to undergo a period of waiting such as attends the marriage of a younger man who is still a dependant in the household of his father.

Although the amount and the value of the marriage gifts offered by a suitor, or on his behalf, are important factors in deciding whether a marriage will be completed, they are by no means decisive. While any girl is flattered to have a high marriage payment made for her, some girls are sufficiently headstrong to insist on marrying a particular suitor whatever the marriage payment. To illustrate this point we give the following quotation from a pre-nuptial conversation between Umaru, a man of about 25 years of age, and Hajo, a girl of about 18 whom he was later to marry. Hajo says,

I love you from now until the day I die. If you were to kill me with a sword, or throw me into a well, I would still love you. However many suitors I may have, it is you whom I love and I will not allow them to marry me. It is you whom I wish to marry me.

At least one other suitor offered to marry Hajo with a higher *tooshi* than that offered by Umaru. She was married to Umaru.

Now since we have noted the conditions or circumstances in which high *tooshi* (roughly over £7) is paid, we should also mention that the middle range of payments (about £2 to £7) covers most marriages to comparatively young women. Finally, the lower range of *tooshi* (from a few shillings to about £2) is of some interest and calls for a few brief comments.

Low *tooshi* payments may be accepted, as we have seen, when the parents of the spouses are close kin; this, in the terminology of some Fulɓe, is the so-called *kogal wuro* ('marriage of the camp'). The low payment expresses the solidarity of the group involved in the marriage or the sentiments of affection between the parents of the spouses. The economic aspects of the union are minimized. As was noted earlier these marriages are comparatively infrequent today.

The greater proportion of low *tooshi* payments is found in those unions in which the women concerned suffer certain disabilities as prospective wives. Among these are older women who are near the menopause, women who are thought to be diseased, reformed prostitutes, barren women, women who are known to be promiscuous and those who are bad tempered, lazy, dirty, and so forth. Since such women have a low marriage value they are not in demand. Payments made for them have not much more than a token value and are made merely—one might suppose—to conform to accepted social usage.

Finally, *tooshi* may be very low among the extremely poor. The suitor, or his representative, simply offers what he can afford. The *tooshi* and *sadaaki* may be only a few pence. The wedding is held in secret under the direction of a *mallam* who reads the *fatiya* in the presence of at least three witnesses. The reason for the secrecy is that people in such marriages are ashamed of their poverty and embarrassed that they are not able to entertain guests.

One other gift is given by or on behalf of the groom to his bride and is called the *ɓangarde* (from the verb *ɓanga*—'to take a wife'). It is given to the bride when she comes to live in her husband's shelter. In 1954 the average value of the *ɓangarde* was estimated to be in the region of from £2 to £4 although the price of some of the items in this gift vary locally and seasonally.

The *ɓangarde* should contain one cloth (or two in the case of a bride's first marriage), which may be of either local or foreign manufacture, together with one head-cloth and one pair of sandals. If it is the bride's first marriage the gift may also include 25 to 50 lb. of corn or rice for her parents and their kin. It is also customary to give the bride a small quantity of henna and kohl—the henna being used to dye her hands and feet and the kohl to paint her eyelids.

When the *sadaaki* and *tooshi* are small gifts the *ɓangarde* is also small. Generous *ɓangarde* is associated with virgin or putatively virgin marriages and with young wives who are remarrying but who are still popular.

These are the principal gifts which are given in marriage. Particulars of a series of marriage gifts are not given, for while the information is at hand, the marriages cover such a time span (about 50 years) that the principles in which we are interested would not be illustrated. However, it is clear from the facts enumerated that for young men, marriages, and especially the first, are comparatively costly, but that the replacement of wives later in life and additional marriages are not expensive. This fact is of some importance in every household in which there are sons, for it affects the conflict between a father and his son as they compete for the resources of the corral in getting married. Less important, though not without significance, is the fact that young wives are expensive to maintain in comparison with older wives, since they insist on being well dressed and generally keeping themselves attractive. A young husband is sensitive to these demands since he knows that early in her marriage his wife's attachment to her conjugal family is weak in comparison with the bond which still holds her to her parental family.

To illustrate these and some other aspects of getting married, an abstract of part of a marriage case history is cited. The case history is of interest also because, as a rule, Fulɓe do not have the patience to discuss a single subject at such length as is required in this type of research.

Case History of a First Marriage

The informant is a man named Manu aged about 23 years (1954).

When Manu was about 4 years old his father died. At the time of his marriage—which was early, 15 years—the informant was living with his elder (by 3 years) married matrilateral half-sister, Satu, and apart from his mother and step-father. Manu married unusually early because of the death of his father, which meant that cattle were available for him and also because Satu complained of too much work and urged Manu to marry so that his wife could help her.

Preliminary arrangements for the marriage were carried out by Satu. She chose a girl, Lame, a year older than Manu and of his clan, but with whom no kinship was traced. Satu went to their mother[1] and said, 'I have chosen a wife for Manu—do you agree?' Manu's mother answered that she did not care, 'I do not wish to have anything to do with it because in the future if Manu quarrels with his wife he will say to his wife that he only married her because it was his mother's wish.'

Satu had told Lame 'when they were young' that she would like her to marry Manu. When Satu asked Manu if he would like to marry Lame he said that he agreed.[2] He had known Lame for some years for they had lived in the same camp. Lame lived with her paternal grandmother. Her father had died and Lame did not like her step-father. Satu got the approval of Lame's paternal grandmother for the marriage.

Manu was 14 years old when he agreed to marry Lame. For at least one Ramadan he gave her about 5s. and a cloth (the gift called *nodirde*, from the verb *noda*, 'call'). During the betrothal he did not 'go to her at night'. If he did the adults of the camp would stop him, *gam ɓe kuli o fechike* (because they feared her genitalia might be torn and this would stop her bearing children in the future).

Manu began to go to the market when he was 14 years of age. Previous to this time he was a *naganaajo* (one who has to herd every day without relief). On his trips to the market he bought kola-nuts (*goro*) for sixpence for Lame. He got the money from Satu who was milking and marketing the milk from his cows. Manu's friend Bele carried the kola-nuts to Lame —'because of shyness I did not carry them myself' (*gam hersa mi yaarai ɗum hore um*). 'The *nordirde* I did take to her myself at the time of play (Ramadan festivities) and she would take it to her shelter and exclaim: Look what I have been given by my Manu!'

---

[1] After the death of his father Manu's mother remarried. However, Manu, when Satu married, chose to live with her and his brother-in-law rather than with his step-father. Hostility between step-father and a step-son is an acknowledged stereotype. Manu says he was afraid that his step-father might poison him.

[2] Owing to the premature death of his father Manu held status and responsibility senior to his years. An unmarried child whose father is dead is called a *chenuɗo* ('holy one' from *sena*, 'be holy'). A *chenuɗo* whether boy or girl is regarded as a spoiled child. Once a boy's father is dead he no longer fears his mother, for on account of his property and the absence of his father he becomes a little household head. Manu's mother had good reason for not advising him in marriage.

Shortly after Manu decided to marry Lame he went to his maternal grandparents (his paternal grandparents were dead) and said, 'I would like to marry Lame, do you agree?' His grandparents did not know her but they asked him, '*o wodi barki?*' ('does she have blessings?'). He answered that her face was not very nice, but she had good character (*gikku*). Then his grandparents said, 'go on with the marriage'. Grandparents sometimes give money for dressing the hair (*cheede moorgol*) or provide food or salt for the wedding, so they should be asked if they approve of the marriage. Manu's grandparents gave nothing.

Manu has one senior paternal half-brother but he was living about 50 miles away and they did not like each other so the brother was not consulted at any stage of the marriage arrangements.

When Manu was 15 he sold a bull for £17; £5 of this he used as *tooshi* for Lame. The *tooshi* was taken by his friend Bele and given to Lame's paternal grandmother.[1] Two days after he gave the *tooshi* Manu's two friends erected a shelter for Lame—unmarried men do not have a shelter.

The *tooshi* was delivered on a Wednesday and on the following Tuesday the *sadaaki* of a heifer was 'shown' to the elders of the camp. On Wednesday the *fatiya* was read. About 30 adult men attended, some of whom were of the same clan as the groom and other men who lived nearby.

The day before the *fatiya* was read both Manu and Lame moved to separate camps (they both lived at the same camp—at which camp the ceremony was held) to stay with friends. Because of 'shyness' they would not stay at the camp where the ceremony is held. Before he went he left 5s. with Bele to buy kola-nuts, *goro kapal kogal* ('kola for tying the marriage'). Friends and kin also contribute a few pennies or a shilling for kola and these are distributed among the wedding guests.

Manu and Lame remained with their friends over Thursday, the day of the *hawrinde kirsil* ('the gathering for the killing'), for shyness is equally felt on this occasion. Manu had instructed Bele which bull (a two year old) was to be killed—it was an animal from Manu's own herd. The carcass of the animal was divided according to a traditional manner and shared among the guests. The animal was not cooked at the site of the ceremony but individuals took it home to cook and eat.[2] Rightful

---

[1] Lame's father had died and her mother remarried and moved off with her husband to wet-season pastures; were it not for this fact the *tooshi* would have been paid to Lame's mother. Apart from the fact that Lame did not like her step-father she stayed behind for her marriage.

[2] The only people expressly forbidden to eat the flesh of the *kirsil* are the bride and groom. It is said that if they eat it when they grow old they will become *bedaiɓe* ('people with the palsy') and people will say, 'look they eat their own *kirsil*, they are gluttons'.

guests who were not present had a portion of meat sent to them. Only snacks, provided by the close kin of both the bride and groom, were served to guests. Young people came from miles around without invitation (for the young invitations are not required) to dance until late in the night.[1]

Manu returned the day after the bull was killed (Friday). On the following Tuesday Satu came to him and said that she would bring back the bride on Thursday. Satu, a girl friend and Bele went on Thursday to collect the bride. When they arrived Satu pretended that she was looking for a goat—then she said she was cold and called out to Lame to bring her a cloth. When Lame entered the shelter to fetch a cloth they blocked the entrance, one of Satu's party brought her the *ɓangarde*. Then they told her that she must go to her shelter at her husband's camp. She said she would not go and began to cry. Then they picked her up and carried her for about 100 yards and let her down, from which point she walked with them to Manu's shelter.

On the night that Lame came to her shelter Manu slept on the ground near his cattle. When he saw that all the people were asleep and the life of the camp was quiet he stole forth to the shelter. He found her asleep and he touched her softly and said, 'you have come today?' and she answered, 'yes'. Then he said, 'move over and give me a place to lie down'. She moved over.

He lay beside her and said how much he liked her. Then she answered the same.

Then he told her the way he wished the marriage to go. He said if any of her kin came to visit her she should give them plenty to eat and he would be happy. But if ever she wished to go away to visit them she should first come to him and he would give her permission. He also said that if she wished to go to the market to sell milk she should first come to see him for his permission.[2]

He told her that when she sells milk she must return early in the evening to prepare his food for he does not like eating food when insects (dung beetles in particular fly about at dusk) have been ground up in it.

Going on he said that if any of his kinsmen or clansmen caused her any trouble—such as scolding her—she should say nothing and come to him and tell him of her problems with them. She was told also to show respect to his parents and to his senior siblings.

[1] Young people may travel 15 miles or more to attend a wedding. Weddings are an important meeting ground for courting.

[2] Manu mentioned in the same account that permission is required only when the camp is small, not more than a few households. The object here is to have at least one individual, if only a child, to stay and 'guard' the household property—domestic animals might get at the food supply.

Next he told her that she must never 'look for' other men, for this he would never tolerate.

After telling her these things he said finally, 'the cattle are here and when we grow old we will give them to our children and they will take care of us'.

They spoke in low whispers for they did not want anyone to know that they were sleeping together. Then he fondled her and consummated the marriage. He found her to be a virgin (*chukudo*) (as in fact he was himself). 'The pleasure of having intercourse with a virgin is like pure honey—a non-virgin is like honey to which water has been added—the sweetness is removed.'

Manu refers to his marriage with Lame as a *kogal yidde* ('marriage of love')—his choice to marry her was ultimately his own and they loved each other. For this reason he was allowed to consummate the marriage on the first night in the shelter. In such marriages there is 'no limit' to the number of times a bride will let her husband have relations with her. He contrasts this type of marriage with the *piɓol* in which there is marriage 'because of the parents' (*gam saarooji*) in which the bride may refuse consummation for a week or more (this is probably an exaggeration of what is found in practice, although it is an explicit ideal).

Manu returned to sleep on the ground by his cattle before the camp stirred.

While the general form of Manu's marriage is typical of first marriages in the community as a whole, it was unusual in certain respects. For example, the premature death of his father was responsible for Manu's early marriage. So long as he was unmarried he held an anomalous position, for while he was the rightful owner of a herd he was dependent on his sister to prepare food and sell milk from his cattle. A herd is a reproductive unit and it should be attached, in the Fulɓe view, to a household which is similarly reproductive. Manu's early marriage is to be seen as initiating the desired unit. Once married he was no longer tied in a frustrating way to the household of his brother-in-law.[1]

Another aspect in which Manu's marriage was atypical was that within a week of the consummation he and his wife (alone) moved

---

[1] According to ideal social usages brothers-in-law (*keeniraaɓe*) should be close friends. However, such friendship is best maintained, in Fulɓe theory, at a distance. There are structural grounds for the vernacular aphorism that, 'if brothers-in-law live together the cattle will not increase'. According to the pastoralists, cattle will increase only when they are attached to a harmonious household and a part of a congenial camp; in practical terms, an efficient household and camp. When brothers-in-law live together there is potential conflict, since 'a man is not happy when he sees his sister dominated by her husband'.

to the wet-season camp and from this time onward his wife took full responsibility as a housewife within his household. Normally, in a first marriage there is a delay, as we shall see, before a viable household comes into existence. But rather than give further details of this specific case history we prefer to describe, in general terms, the manner in which a woman is socially and economically integrated into her conjugal family and a new family household is thereby founded.

12

THE HUSBAND-WIFE RELATIONSHIP

IN Fulɓe marriage, as in other societies, there are certain structural constants despite individual variation—differences of temperament, personal habits, and so forth.

The character of the relations between spouses varies according to the stage of their marital career and, in a general way, the fortunes of their marriage.

We are here concerned with the broad features of structural behaviour between spouses (and to a lesser extent with their respective affines), but obviously not all marriages conform in every detail to the pattern which we have outlined. Fulɓe themselves are adept at describing how a man and his wife should behave towards each other, but they realize that the ideal is rarely, if ever, fully attained in practice, and they are prepared to accept a degree of deviation.

When a young man marries for the first time he does not, unless his father is old or infirm, immediately establish a separate household. He remains under the authority of his father and his wife becomes a helper to his mother. Neither spouse has an immediate increase in responsibility as a result of marriage. A man carries out the same tasks under his father as he did before his marriage and instead of being a helper to her mother a bride is a helper to her mother-in-law. A bride has her own shelter in which she is visited by her husband at night, but, unlike the shelter of a wife whose husband is a household head, it does not contain milk calabashes and household utensils, a housewife's symbol of economic responsibility.

When she is newly married a wife is a sort of housewife apprentice, although she already knows much of the work of women and will give valuable assistance to her mother-in-law (referred to as *esirao* ('in-law') but addressed as 'mother', or as 'my mother', *inna* and *innaum* respectively). For her mother-in-law a young wife will fetch firewood and water, churn, spin, grind corn, and help with the cooking. She may also milk, but this is comparatively rare since it is more likely to be done by either her husband or her father-in-law[1] (referred to as *esirao*, but addressed as 'father', *baba*).

Early in her marriage a woman must be especially circumspect with regard to her behaviour for she lives in close contact with her affines. Towards all her seniors she should be modest, shy, and obedient. The fact that she is of the same sex as her mother-in-law and that they co-operate in household tasks serves to lessen the reserve between them. But the generation difference always functions to maintain a degree of social distance in their relationship. Ideally, the relationship, although reciprocally described as an 'in-law avoidance' (*esiraagu*, from *esirao*, 'in-law') should, in the course of time, according to the Fulɓe, come to resemble a 'mother–daughter' (*latike ɓiɗɗo*, 'become an offspring') pattern of behaviour. Respect should always be shown to the mother-in-law because 'she bore her (the daughter-in-law's) husband' (*o rimi gorko makko*).[2] Any milk-maid knows how important it is to get on well with her mother-in-law because a son always pays careful attention to his mother's opinion of his wife; the mother–son (and daughter) link is very strong.

Early in her marriage a woman does not get to know her father-in-law well from direct social contact since there is a stricter avoidance relation between them and their social and economic activities do not bring them into contact as do those of a woman and her mother-in-law. In the opinion of some Fulɓe a man should never speak and does not speak to his daughter-in-law;[3] others do not place so great an emphasis on not speaking provided

[1] Milking is the one task in which there is not a clear-cut division of labour according to sex. A majority of both men and women know how to milk. As a rule, however, men prefer to milk because they feel that since women do not have the interest of the herd at heart they will not leave enough milk for the calves. Moreover, some cattle are extremely restive and often women are nervous about milking them.

[2] That this ideal is in fact taken seriously may be illustrated in Manu's case history (cited above). In the first year of Manu's marriage his mother came to stay with him and his wife. On one occasion Lame (his wife) insulted her mother-in-law and called her 'useless'. The latter replied, 'but how can I be useless, did I not bear your Manu?' Manu was so upset by the incident that, 'my heart was removed from her' (i.e. he no longer 'loved' her, *ɓernde um itike i makko*). Indeed, he was so incensed that he was afraid he might beat her violently and so be called before the *alkali*. Rather than have this happen he divorced her.

[3] A daughter-in-law and son-in-law are referred to (M. and F. S.) as *esirao* and may be addressed by name. Some Fulɓe, however, say, *hey ahan* ('hey you') when addressing a child-in-law.

the other avoidances are observed. These are: not sitting on the same bed or sleeping mat, not eating together, keeping the body modestly covered in each other's presence and avoiding being in the same shelter at the same time.

Much more could, of course, be said on the subject of avoidance among affines, but we have only enough space to note certain of the more important principles. Avoidance is most strongly emphasized shortly after marriage, that is, when the spouses and their parents are still young. It is less and less marked as the people involved in the relationship grow older. When parents are approaching or have reached senility it may be difficult for an observer to notice avoidance behaviour, although a vestige (if only a name avoidance) remains. Because of the dominance of viri-local and neo-local residence a man probably does not see his parents-in-law frequently. In such social contacts as he does have with them, however, he observes the same pattern of behaviour as his wife observes towards her parents-in-law. Avoidance is strictest towards his mother-in-law, but when his parents-in-law grow old his relations with them are relaxed.

The fact that when they first marry spouses do not immediately form a household means that the transition to their new status is not abrupt. Indeed, some parents object to their daughter marrying a man who has previously wed because it is then likely that she will at once have to assume the full responsibility of a housewife in a viable household. When the preferred pattern is followed—a girl marrying a man who is marrying for the first time—she can remain relatively carefree until she has borne her first child.

After a bride has begun to live with her bridegroom there is no attempt to delay her immediate pregnancy, either on her part or that of her husband, for they are both anxious to have children. Spouses know that marriage ties are most tenuous until there is pregnancy and ultimately a child. If spouses are happy together they are especially glad to learn that they are to have a child since this will strengthen their affection for each other; each feeling that the other has fulfilled his or her marital function. But they do not allow their delight over a first pregnancy to show in their deportment, for they are shy 'because they are still children'. More than shyness they feel a sort of temporary maladjustment, for while they are not yet parents they are not truly children. They are in a transitional phase between childhood and adulthood.

In her pregnancy a woman feels more shy than her husband and she endeavours to keep her condition a secret as long as possible although her husband is likely soon to learn that she has ceased menstruating. No gifts are given to a wife as a formal recognition of her pregnancy, but a good husband should and often does improve her diet by bringing her meat and ground-nut cakes from the market. Sexual relations continue during the pregnancy until a period which varies locally from the fourth to the seventh month of gestation, when the wife returns to her maternal homestead.[1] The return to the mother's homestead is not marked by ceremonial or ritual; indeed, the young wife may, by leaving early in the morning, return without the knowledge of her husband and his kin. Since a husband does not found a household prior to the birth of his first child his wife's return to her maternal homestead does not disrupt his domestic requirements.

The period during which a wife remains at the homestead of her mother after the birth of her first child varies. Most informants say that a mother should stay two years in her maternal home (in addition to the latter months of her pregnancy) and then return alone, leaving the child with its maternal grandmother. In practice a wife usually returns to her conjugal family within a year after having given birth to her child bringing the infant with her.[2] The initiative for the return of the wife is taken by the husband who goes to the home of his mother-in-law with gifts which together are called the *bantirde* and include a cloth, a pair of sandals, and perhaps a gift of 10s. or more. It may also include 2s. 'money for dressing the hair' (*cheede moorgol*). The change of status of the wife in virtue of her childbirth is now seen in the fact that when she returns she is equipped with the 'things of a housewife' (*kaidu yeyaajo*, household utensils and calabashes)[3] and perhaps several head of cattle given to her by her father.

The return of the wife to the home of her husband with her

---

[1] The timing of the 'return for childbirth' (*bomgal*) varies according to clan background and to expedience. In essentials the childbirth complex is similar among all Fulɓe of Gwandu but there are differences in details. A detailed discussion of these differences lies beyond the scope of this paper.

[2] The post-Protectorate dispersal of clans and the modern freedom of movement has strongly influenced, and in some cases made impracticable, the traditional practice of a wife and her child spending a long period with her mother. It will be remembered that in the 'Time of War' the parents of any two spouses were co-residential in the clan-village.

[3] Provided by her mother from the *tooshi*.

child marks a crucial stage in household development. Now for the first time her shelter is equipped with utensils which she places in an orderly and traditional manner according to her observations and instructions in the shelter of her mother. In describing this stage of household development Fulɓe say that she has been given (by her husband) a 'utensil platform' (*danki*),[1] which is symbolic of a stage in her advancing status as a housewife. Bearing a child has made her an adult and providing her with a *danki* is an expression of this fact.[2]

Receiving her *danki* brings an advance in status to a wife which is paralleled by a similar advance in the status of her husband. When a wife returns to her husband her father-in-law removes cattle from his own herd and gives them to her husband. Henceforth these beasts—together with the wife's cattle, if any—occupy a separate place in front of the shelter of the young couple. The calves, in order to control their suckling, are tied (in order of their birth)[3] to a rope stretched between the shelter and the new herd. Thus a basic economic unit comes into existence even though the spatial separation from the homestead of the father may be but a few yards. There will still be co-operation between the father and his son and the young wife may still give assistance to her mother-in-law. There is, however, much symbolic significance in the fact that the young husband each evening lights his own corral fire to which he calls his cattle, he has his own calf-rope and his wife has

[1] A *danki* may be given in advance of the birth of a first child, if, for example, as in Manu's marriage, the father died prematurely and Manu required (since his mother lived elsewhere) a housewife.

[2] The first child born to a man and his wife is called an *afo* and the succeeding children are called *didabo, tatabo, naiabo*, &c. (second, third, fourth, &c.). Parents strictly observe name-avoidance of their *afo*, male or female. There is a degree of variation in pattern of name avoidance which is linked to the heterogeneous clan background of the population of the community. For example, some parents extend the avoidance to the first two or more children—one parent extended it to the first five. It would take me beyond the scope of this report to write in detail of this type of avoidance, but it should be noted that most males, in particular, would like to be the first-born. The last-born in a woman's reproductive cycle is also known by a special term *autaajo* (H. *auta*). His status may be envied since he is pampered by his parents, but this is counter-balanced by his comparatively harsh treatment by his elder siblings.

[3] No explanation was given for this practice. It may be interpreted as symbolically representing the importance of seniority. However, a practical advantage of the custom is that it is safer for the young calves; by this method the oldest calves (two years) and the youngest (several days) are at the extreme ends of the rope.

her own household fire and her own utensil platform. The young spouses are now clearly in a position of ascending importance *vis-à-vis* the young herdsman's parents. Moreover, when a wife receives her utensil platform and her husband receives his herd economic partnership between the spouses begins and their social relations with each other intensify. This is necessarily so since together they must now supervise a herd and from its resources gain their own subsistence.

Until he has a son of 7 years of age or older a man is likely to remain with his father and their cattle will be taken to pasture as a joint herd—attended by the married son (if he is an only son) or by his junior brothers. Thus it is seen that when a man has only infant children he still co-operates with his father (or younger brothers) in herding duties. But even though he may reside near and co-operate with his father, a man is economically independent so far as the management of his own household is concerned. Out of the combined income from the sale of stock increase and of dairy products he and his wife will get their food and clothing and meet other expenses of their household. He will no longer expect to receive either food or clothing from the income of the herd of the father. A young married man who is still living with his father and whose income from the sale of dairy products is not adequate will first tell his father if he intends to sell stock. This is a subtle way of suggesting that the father should give him more cattle, for no man likes to see healthy beasts, either his own or those of his son, sold.

At this stage we do not detail the father–son relationship since a fuller discussion of that subject is given below. But it is necessary to mention that even when a man has infant children he still, to some extent, defers to his father. He has been conditioned from childhood to show respect for his father and this attitude is not abandoned abruptly, if indeed it is abandoned at all, until the father has reached such an age that he has handed over all his cattle to his sons.

In considering some aspects of the pattern of relations between a man and his wife it should be noted first that the husband is the unquestioned head of the household. There are numerous day-to-day expressions of this fact in the social intercourse between a man and his wife, which are obvious even to the casual observer. For example, when a wife brings food to her husband she kneels on the ground before him and, holding the calabash in both hands, gently places it at his feet. Having given him his food she leaves him quickly so that she will not see him eat. As a further sign of respect she does not address her husband by name and in most conversations she does not speak until she is spoken to. She usually replies to her husband with a quiet and respectful tone such as that used by a minor when speaking to an adult. A wife must show her obedience by bringing her husband drinking water, a sleeping mat, items of clothing, and so forth whenever he desires. In these and in numerous other ways a wife shows respect and obedience towards her husband. There are few husbands who will tolerate disobedient and disrespectful conduct on the part of a wife, and when it is seen in practice it is an almost infallible sign that the marriage is not going well. However, it should be noted that the formality of the husband–wife relationship relaxes, to some extent, through the years, for in those marriages which endure the spouses have developed a mutual affection. Moreover, as a wife bears children she tends to be regarded less by her husband as a personal servant for he knows that her children make demands on her time and energy. A woman who has borne children can afford to be rather offhand with her husband since, in virtue of her children, she is much less likely to be divorced than if she were childless. In bearing children a wife has produced an asset equal in value to the herd upon which the household depends. But no matter how long a woman has been married to her husband or how admirably she has fulfilled her role as a housewife, she can never hope to become his equal and she must always defer to him to some extent. Near, but not absolute, social equality between spouses comes only with old age when they live as dependants on their children. But so long as a man commands a herd he demands the subordination of his wife (and children). In the Fulɓe view, in the management of a household, the demands of the herd come first, so it follows that he who is in charge of the herd must also have the superior voice in the management of the household. A man's unquestioned authority in his own household is supported by the value and legal systems of the Islamic community as a whole (Fulɓe and Haaɓe) and by the herdsmen's sincere belief that women are innately of inferior intelligence. This view is often put forward in many stereotyped expressions which stress not only the inferior intelligence of women, but also their malicious character. When these expressions are used it is almost always in a context in which wives are being discussed—not, for example, one's mother or sister. It would be a novice, indeed, among Fulɓe men and youths who had not heard almost to the point of tedious repetition these numerous invectives about women.

Undoubtedly the frequent repetition of such expressions has an important function in contributing to the social segregation of men and women. Married men are thoroughly conscious of the fact that, if they associate with their wives more than is necessary, they may lose their authority over them. They will also lose status among their age fellows, and there is also a fear that by a sort of contamination a man's outlook may become adversely affected— 'his talk[1] (outlook) resembles that of a housewife' (i.e. he talks nonsense) (*haala makko ki nandi haala yeyaajo*). Such a comment is extremely uncomplimentary—as one might expect—and it is doubtful if it would ever be made to a man's face.

In addition, men are not interested in the company of women because their spheres of activities diverge. From the time when they are little boys, Fulɓe are told that their interests are cattle and little girls are told that they should be interested in the 'shelter'. Thus training and practice in household activities along sexual lines further separate the fields of interest of men and women. But the end result is an extremely efficient household organization where each member has no doubt as to the tasks which he or she must perform. It should be noted, however, that just as a husband and wife do not spend their leisure time together, especially when young, so also their household work does not bring them into prolonged face to face contact. We would estimate that, apart from time spent on their sleeping mat, spouses spend on an average between one and two hours each day within a few yards of each other. And as a rule only for a fraction of this time do they engage in conversation. However, in the relations between a husband and wife an important change is now taking place; today, since homesteads exist either in complete isolation or in very small clusters, men cannot always find age-mates with whom to share their leisure at the camp. In consequence the free time may, on occasion,

---

[1] In the above context the word 'talk' (*haala*) may be limited in its reference to the outlook of the man, but it may also refer to his actual speech, for Fulɓe recognize a slightly different dialect and vocabulary in the speech of men and women. I mention this not only as an interesting sociological point, but also as a problem which may be of interest to linguists.

be spent with their respective wives. This may have some bearing on the fact that men today prefer to choose their own wives in the hope of finding temperamental compatibility, and it may also partially explain why today women no longer 'fear' their husbands. In short, though men much prefer the companionship of other men to that of their wives, today, because local groups are small, they spend more time with their wives than did their forebears. Nevertheless, it should be remembered that men may spend almost their entire day in the nearby Haaɓe villages where they associate very largely with Fulɓe and almost exclusively with their own sex.

While, as we have noted, pastoralists are strongly opposed to social equality between spouses, there is the accepted value that the husband should not be a despot. However, the fact that he is the undisputed household head gives him, what in the herdsmen's view he must have, considerable authority over his wife. She must obey all his reasonable commands, account to him for her movements and submit to his wishes in household affairs. He has a monopoly of her sexual favours, which, of course, is not reciprocal since polygynous marriage is approved. Children born of a union come under the authority of the father just as their mother does. Should there be a divorce, infant children may remain with their mother in the household of their step-father. But when a male child reaches six or seven years of age his father claims custody of him. Female children are normally permitted to stay with their mother (which is their preference) until they are wed. But the father as well as the mother, is entitled to decide the choice of a daughter's husband and to receive a share of the marriage gifts; but in many cases for convenience (owing to spatial separation) the rights in both are voluntarily surrendered.

So far we have stressed the authority aspect of a man's relations with his wife, but as in other societies he also has very specific obligations towards her. Perhaps his most onerous responsibility is that of supporting her adequately. If his wife does not receive enough milk from which to secure a sufficient income for the household then he must either sell stock or provide corn from his farm. An amiable and efficient wife may provide clothing for herself, her husband, and her children, but should she refuse to do so (either through inability or lack of inclination) he will be obliged again to sell stock.

Although a man is the household authority and his social contact with his wife is minimal, he is expected to protect her and to treat her with kindly consideration. He is expected to exercise his authority in an extreme degree (for instance, by thrashing her) only when she obviously and deliberately fails to fulfil her obligations toward him. When a man's wife is over-tired or ill he should forgive what may appear to be inefficiency. If his wife is depressed he should console her and if she is in difficulty with other people he should support her. When a wife is ill her husband should find medicine for her. He should make frequent gifts of kola-nuts and every month or two give her money (about 2s.) for dressing her hair. Women (and men also) take great pride in their personal appearance, especially when they visit a market, and they often lose patience with a husband who does not have enough resources—or is too stingy with them—to allow them to indulge their vanity. It would hardly be an exaggeration to say that women regard gifts from their husbands as the only genuine assurance of the latter's affection and appreciation.

While a man is the master of the household he does not interfere, nor should he, with his wife's management of her domestic affairs provided she does her work efficiently. It is almost a positive masculine virtue to know little or nothing about the 'work of women'. For example, it would be a rare breach of etiquette for a man to inquire of his wife as to the cash return from the sale of dairy products. She may volunteer the information, especially during times of shortage when she may have difficulty in feeding her family and may desire help from her husband. But if her income from the sale of milk and butter is greater than her expenditure she is not required to report this to her husband. In Fulɓe theory the husband's concern should be that he receive enough food as well prepared as living conditions and the season permit, but no man should question the details of his wife's income and spending. Marriage case histories clearly indicate that between spouses there are on occasion serious disputes in which the husband accuses his wife of not being sufficiently frugal in the use of her resources and of being unskilled in marketing. However, when the income of a household is small it is the housewife who consumes the least so that her husband and children may be relatively well fed; or so it is when she wishes to remain with her husband.

A point which must be mentioned, and which colours the relationship between spouses, is the fact that divorce can be easily obtained and, as a rule, a young woman can obtain a spouse more easily than can a man of any age. It is the ease of divorce which mitigates the treatment which a man might otherwise give his wife and the marital demand for young wives which inclines the latter not to tolerate a marriage in which their life is too oppressive. That is to say, a husband, especially if he heads a monogamous household and even if he heads a polygynous household, is restrained in his demands on his wife since frequent divorce (or desertion) and re-marriage involve expense, are time-consuming, and generally disrupt the activities of his household. For these reasons a man cannot afford to initiate or provoke the termination of his marriage impulsively, and indeed, not infrequently, a man must put up with a disagreeable wife for some months until he can arrange a remarriage, for as we have seen a viable household must include at least one housewife. Women recognize the value of remaining with one husband for their lifetime, and especially if there are children; but women have little compunction in deserting if they feel that their rights are being infringed or that they can improve their marital fortunes elsewhere. Restitution of conjugal rights is not enforced by the courts and when, as happens occasionally, it is attempted outside the court (as in the case of Satu, p. 76, above) it is rarely successful.

Thus it is clear that, although the husband is the master of his household, he must be circumspect in his behaviour lest his wife desert him. Today, unlike the past, women are no longer confined to their own living quarters and their regular visits to nearby villages give them opportunities not only to compare their lot with other women but also to meet potential husbands. A woman who, as a result of her gossip in the market-place, feels that other women have married better than she, and who at the same time has had offers of marriage, has to be treated well by her husband if she is to remain with him. Moreover, modern women meeting *en masse* in the markets (a post-Protectorate development) have begun to realize how vital they are in the pastoral economy, and this gives them a sense of power *vis-à-vis* their husbands. Husbands also know that if they do not treat their wives fairly it will become common knowledge over a wide area within a short time, because women spend 5 to 7 hours a day in the markets for several days during the week.

An important feature of Fulɓe marriage is that although spouses

admit an affection for each other—which is rarely openly demonstrated—the fact remains that the husband-wife tie is a weak one in
comparison with that between a parent and its child, especially a
mother and her children. On an average marriages will endure for
about two years if they are childless—or if there is no pregnancy in
this interval. In some cases spouses part on good terms both
regretting that they were unable to produce children and mutually
agreeing that they should marry elsewhere. In other cases frustration over childlessness causes violent arguments which precipitate
divorce. When infertility is suspected the husband or the wife or
both may try to remedy the condition by taking 'medicine of child-
birth' (*magani dimgal*), a herbal concoction which they may prepare
themselves or which they procure from the Haaɓe. So much value
is placed on fertility that neither men nor women like to admit to
themselves that they are infertile—much less to anyone else.

The life of those unfortunate individuals who cannot reproduce
is one of misery and, as they grow older, they view with envy
their age fellows who have children. A man who is sterile (*d'ingineejo*,
pl. *d'ingineeɓe*) may be unaware of the fact or may conceal it for
some time; often such individuals may marry up to ten times in
their lifetime. Some case histories are a record of an almost frantic
struggle to beget children and/or the impatience of their successive
wives. The man who is impotent (*la'ifiijo*, pl. *la'ifii'en*, also *wala
kaiya*, i.e. 'without genitalia') is in an even more trying position
since, of course, his condition cannot be concealed if he marries.
However, it is unlikely that such men will marry at all because they
are aware of their condition before they consider marriage. Only
one instance of the marriage of an impotent man was recorded and
in that case the wife absconded within a few days. Impotent men
usually seek wage labour in the cities or become shepherds. In both
cases their condition is not likely to attract as much attention and
occasion as much embarrassment as it would were they to remain
with their kinsfolk.

Women who are barren (*tonotoodo*, pl. *tonotooɓe*) like their
male counterparts usually contract a series of short-lived marriages
in which they are often harshly treated since they fail to fulfil the
most important role in marriage. The reaction of women to their
misfortune varies from individual to individual. But always their
future is insecure and they feel that they are rather outside the
society. The more fortunate of these women marry men who are

widowed and who have had children by a former wife. Barren women are said to be and are the best step-mothers. Of his union with a barren woman a herdsman said, 'We have been together (married) for 17 years, she has not borne children, but she takes good care of my children and I like her'. Some barren women, in order to spite their husbands who have treated them harshly, or having given up hope of marrying happily, abandon the pastoral society and become prostitutes. Still others earn a living in the towns by retailing milk[1] and butter and, in their spare time, spinning cotton and engaging in prostitution.

It will now be appreciated that childless adults occupy an anomalous position in the community and indeed, as we have seen, some of them leave the society altogether. The urgency of bearing children lies in the fact that it is only on one's children (and sons in particular) that an individual can depend throughout his or her life. For example, a man who has a step-son can count on the latter leaving him probably at the age of 7 to return to his patri-kin. Even if he is without these kin a step-son is certain to leave at his marriage and he will most likely take his mother with him. The antipathy between a step-father and a step-son is a Fulɓe stereotype and the attitude has the sanction of a myth.[2]

There is no provision whereby a man without a son may adopt one. Parents deem it unthinkable to give up rights to their own children and orphan children remain either with their senior siblings or their parents' siblings—boys with their older brothers or their father's brothers and girls with their mother's sisters.

We have digressed from our theme of the behaviour between spouses only to indicate the practical necessity of marriages being productive of children (sons in particular). This necessity arises from the fact that there is no really satisfactory means by which a

[1] Whenever possible pastoral housewives themselves sell the milk which they carry to the villages. However, the time which a housewife can spend in a market may not always be sufficient for her to sell all the milk, for not infrequently they walk ten or more miles to market. In these circumstances they may sell the milk to a retailer (*chooko*, pl. *sookooɓe*) who, being a village resident, may go on selling into the night. Because of work at their homesteads and their husband's suspicions Fulɓe women rarely stay overnight in the villages.

[2] It is said that Shefu, the leader of the Jihad had a step-son. The story goes on to say that the step-son (un-named) knew the place where Shefu went to pray, and in this place he buried a knife with the point uppermost just below the surface. Shefu discovered the knife and he knew that the step-son had intended him injury. He cursed his step-son and from that time, it is believed, step-sons have been 'without blessings'.

sonless household head can manage his household and make adequate provision for the future. Men are strongly averse from acting as pater for a child of which they are not (or believe themselves not to be) also the genitor. The custom in certain societies, whereby a sterile man may arrange for a friend or kinsman to impregnate his wife, was regarded by those who were told of it as revolting. However, since women today have considerable freedom of movement, it seems likely that some of their surreptitious affairs, thus made possible, arise from a desire for impregnation when they suspect that their husbands are sterile. It is impossible to get precise information on this point, but its occurrence is suggested by the reproductive histories of men.

Having noted some aspects of the social consequences of infertility we may now discuss the various factors which give rise to conflicts in marriages in which there are children. This is, of course, a vast subject and we cannot attempt to give it exhaustive treatment here. Nevertheless there are certain important principles at work in Fulɓe marriage which can be indicated briefly.

At the outset it should be noted that the vicissitudes of pastoral life carry certain hazards to contentment in marriage. Not all men and women adjust and react equally to the hardship and recurrent crises of their existence. During the wet season, because of inadequate or no shelters, men, women, and children are often cold and wet and do not sleep well. In the dry season milk is scarce so that often there is not enough food to 'satisfy' the members of the household. It is at this time in particular that tempers are short and incidents which might otherwise be considered trivial become the cause of violent argument. Men, especially, become sullen and uncommunicative, for in addition to being under-nourished themselves, they are worried about the same condition in their herd. Added to this, at the height of the dry season night herding is at its maximum and, as this is usually done by the household heads, the extra fatigue further shortens their tempers.

Though the wet season has its discomforts, women, like the men, regard the dry season as the most trying. It is said that this is the time when a woman weighs the possibilities of marrying elsewhere or returning to her mother, where she may receive more food. However, if a woman has children her interests are more strongly identified with her marital household and she will withstand more hardship than a childless mother. A woman's life is strenuous in the dry season because she, perhaps even more than the rest of the family, lives on a meagre diet while her work is increased, since more corn (which is difficult to prepare) is consumed at this season than in the wet season when milk is relatively abundant. In the dry season too a housewife lives under more psychological strain than in the wet season because of the bad temper of her husband and her worry that she is not feeding her family well enough.

Another aspect of the discomfort of an unkindly habitat is the necessity for the seasonal movement of the household and its herd. Herd-owners strongly resent interference from their wives as to where and when to move, but in this respect women are by no means neutral. For example, on more than one occasion we have seen a herd-owner leave a good herding area because his wife could not get on with other women of the camp. In these cases, when spatial separation is desired, the move may be only a mile or two. A housewife may also complain if favourable markets or the domestic water supply are too far from the homestead. There are women, too, who quickly become lonely and may be afraid at night (mostly of hyenas) and they induce their husbands to join other households or, very exceptionally, to take a second wife. Finally, a woman, especially when she is young, objects strongly to a move which will take her far from her close kin—particularly if she feels that she will be separated from them for a long time.[1] A young wife has strong ties with members of her natal family and she looks to them for protection and advice, especially until she has her own children and has come to trust her husband. Evidence on this point is provided by a number of recorded cases in which a rather long move (upwards of 50 miles) was planned and the wife returned to her mother rather than follow her husband. Similarly, a wife's parents may make a long move and induce their daughter to return to them.

It is obvious, therefore, that although decisions of seasonal movement and migration rest with the herd-owner he cannot be entirely arbitrary in his choice if he hopes to have a contented wife. This is especially the case when a wife is young, that is, when her

---

[1] Without going into too much detail I should mention that parents will accept the fact that their daughter may be separated from them for more than 50 miles for a season. But they may object (as also may the daughter) if the separation continues for several seasons and appears as though it may become permanent.

PLATE III

Girls make model camps and stock them with miniature calabashes

PLATE IV

Fulɓe women sell milk in a small market
Photo. Dr. N. A. Barnicot

ties with her close kin are still strong, when she does not yet 'know' (i.e. is unaccustomed to) her husband and when she knows that if she deserts she will have little difficulty in remarrying.

Thus we see that the ecology and natural habitat tend to produce stresses and tensions in marriage. These are at a maximum so long as spouses are childless, for until there are children a husband and wife tend to be selfish in their interests. A wife without children is mainly interested in receiving good food and clothing and gaining the assurance of the affection of her husband. A husband, on the other hand, tends to be less interested in short-term objectives but more concerned about the efficient maintenance of his herd and securing their increase. This is a man's constant objective throughout his active life and all his other interests are subordinated to it. Real enthusiasm about the welfare of the household herd is acquired by a wife only gradually as, through circumspect behaviour and the rearing of children, she integrates herself into her marital household. The bearing of a child, especially a son, marks a tangible and necessary stage in the integration of a housewife into the household of her husband. From this point forward she begins to become more selfless, she has more confidence that her marriage will endure and in consequence begins to share more fully in the interests of her husband—the primacy of the herd. In bearing children she has produced legal heirs (see 'Inheritance', p. 139) through whose filial regard her future is assured—provided the prosperity of the household is maintained.

Through having children a housewife becomes less dependent on her husband for affection just as she will rely less on the affection of her parents. Year by year, as her children grow older and take on increased responsibilities and as her sons acquire greater influence, a housewife gains in status. Because her sons have such a high regard for her, her husband dare not treat her too harshly lest he lose their support upon which he depends more and more as he and they grow older.

The prospect of a secure and relatively care-free old age under the care of their sons will often restrain young women from deserting or divorcing their husbands. Both men and women in many respects show a remarkable disposition to forego present convenience (or pleasure) in the interests of future benefit. In this connexion it should be noted that in general the Fulɓe have an almost pathological concern (and often fear) for the future. Their conversation abounds with expressions such as, '*to jaango?*' ('what of tomorrow?') and '*gam jaango*' ('because of tomorrow'). These are used when they are questioning the wisdom of a proposed action or justifying a completed action, respectively. They are in fact very much concerned about the relationship between present behaviour and future consequences—upon which they hold many and lengthy deliberations. Although we mention this fact in the context of marriage it should be kept in mind as an important general theme in the society and, moreover, it is a principle about which they are notably self-conscious and which they uphold as a specific Fulɓe virtue.

There seems little question that if they did not concern themselves for the future, women would be much less tolerant of the various irksome tasks and incidents of marriage. Women say—and this more or less influences their behaviour—that it is unwise to marry too often, for in all marriages women have to exercise patience (*munyal*), i.e. all marriages are much the same from a woman's point of view. And in frequent marriages one's future is jeopardized. There is also the point, of which they are fully aware, that when spouses have been together for a long time they come to know each other's temperament and expectations and in general the household runs more smoothly and less strenuously. Men, too, have often mentioned that, while they do not have a special affection for their wives, they have come to know each other, *min boowi* (accustomed to each other's ways) and for this reason they have stayed together. The household organization is a conservative one and great value is placed on the harmonious co-operation of the members. Women, no less than men, are disturbed by the necessary mutual adjustment of spouses early in their marriage.

To summarize some of the more important factors which concern us:[1]

The stereotype of the husband and wife relationship is one of discipline-respect. Difference in status between spouses is most pronounced early in marriage, but through the years this gap slowly narrows until finally in their old age they become dependent upon

[1] Since detailed and quantitative material is at hand I propose in a later paper to give a more comprehensive analysis of this subject. For example, the scheme of the present paper does not permit me to discuss this very complicated interplay of Fulɓe traditions and the District courts on the question of divorce and desertion. I hope also to give the incidence of divorce and desertion and to weigh the contributing causes.

their sons. In old age the status difference is slight for in this age group sex differences are of little consequence.

The status of a married woman in her household increases according to the degree to which, through her behaviour and child-bearing, she has discharged her functions and contributed (through her children) to the present and future fortunes of that household.

Early in their marriage women are of comparatively low status because so far they have 'brought nothing' (*wadai komi*) (or contributed nothing) and they are consequently dispensable. It is, as it were, as if they are on probation and only through time can they prove their worth. In contrast the 'contribution' of the husband in founding a household is immediate: he has provided the marriage gifts and from his herd he provides food and clothing. In other words, he has already proved his worth. He has provided the foundation of the household and, in pastoral theory, it is only fitting that he should be its unquestioned head.

A woman advances in the esteem of her husband as she bears children—especially sons[1]—and, because of her influence over her sons, she advances in status as their responsibility increases.

Finally it should be noted that a husband knows that he cannot demand too much of his wife or she will desert him and/or get a divorce. On the other hand, a woman is prepared to defer to her husband since she knows that such is the traditional lot of women, and also that there are long term advantages in remaining married to one husband, or at most, limiting the number of marriages in her lifetime.

---

[1] Although parents favour having sons rather than daughters the preference is rarely verbalized. I could not get a concrete reason for this reticence, but I believe that they feel that if they were to complain that they bore only daughters then the gift of reproduction might—as a sort of supernatural revenge—be withdrawn entirely: 'who knows the ways of Allah?'

13

RELATIONSHIPS BETWEEN FATHER AND SON AND BETWEEN BROTHERS

SINCE among the Fulɓe the agnatic principle is of prime significance, the behaviour patterns found among fathers, sons, and brothers are crucial to our analysis. It is our main task in this section to show that the details of behaviour among these categories of kin will vary according to the stage of development of any household. It is, of course, obvious that in the relations between a father and his son a number of factors influence the nature of the behaviour between them. One of the most important of these is their individual temperaments, a phenomenon which cannot easily be explained wholly in structural terms. While most fathers manage to receive devotion and close co-operation from their sons, some are anything but successful in this respect.

If an outside observer were to ask a Pullo the 'correct' behaviour of a son towards his father he would doubtless receive the answer: 'give him respect' (*tendaniimo*, lit. 'give heaviness' or, *hokka maungu*, lit. 'give greatness'). If the observer were to see a father and son together he would usually gather from their behaviour that the ideal was carried out in practice. It is an important principle of the pastoral society that an individual must, at least in public, show respect not only to his father but also to all members of the parental generation whether or not they are kinsmen or clansmen. But whatever the formality of conduct and the façade of etiquette, the fact remains that conflicts between a father and son do exist—though they may vary in intensity, and we shall attempt to show that to some extent conflict is inherent in the process of household development.

In considering the father–son relationship our analysis can be more refined if we consider not only the age difference between the father and son but also their respective chronological ages, for an individual's experience, capabilities, interests, and ambitions vary according to his age. Now the relations between a man who is say 30 years of age and his son aged 10 are quite different from the relations between a father and son whose age discrepancy is 20 years but whose ages are 40 and 20 respectively. Ample evidence can be produced to show that, in the first case the behaviour between father and son most closely approximates to the ideal held in society. At the age of 10 a boy looks to his father as a man whose authority cannot be questioned and, provided the son does not suffer ill health, he can be counted on to herd the cattle every day, if necessary.[1] A lad at this age would not dare refuse to herd, except on account of illness, and still remain in the camp of his father. When a boy is very young the relative age of his father is not significant. His father is an adult to whom he must accord respect, and the herd-boy has a clearly defined duty to herd when he is told to do so. Even if a young boy (up to the age of 13 or 14) is free of herding duties he is rarely permitted to visit Haaße villages as do older youths and adults, so this is not a distraction for him.

Thus, from the point of view of the father, the conflict with a son is least intense when the latter is under the age of about 14 years, and he can rely on such a son to carry out his commands. But after this age it is the rule, rather than the exception, that tension between the father and son begins to increase. Boys of this age and upwards tend to object to continuous herding duties since they wish to visit the villages to meet their age-fellows and their girl friends. A boy of 14 or more is in a favourable bargaining position because he is old enough to leave his home and seek employment elsewhere if he objects to the treatment given to him in his father's household. The existence of an outside labour market is a post-Protectorate development the importance of which must be stressed, for it has undermined the father–son authority structure.

It will be remembered that in the 'Time of War' an individual's entire life and future was centred in a clan-village. Owing to the insecurity of the period it was unthinkable for an individual to leave alone and on his own initiative. Furthermore, the larger local groupings meant that in any crisis situation a youth faced the concerted opinion of a group of men of the parental generation. In

---

[1] However, during the research period two instances occurred, to my knowledge, in which herd-boys (ages about 10 and 12, and, incidently, senior sons) let it be known that they felt they were given too strenuous herding duties by leaving their fathers' households and going to stay at the household of their mothers' brothers. In both cases these were at distances of between 20 and 30 miles. For the very young this is the only sanction which is applied to one's father. In both cases the fathers simply went and got their sons and brought them back, but not without some embarrassment and the fatigue of a long journey.

these circumstances, unlike today, revolt against parental authority was unthinkable.

To modern youths a village (and the larger the better) presents a great attraction in contrast to the long, lonely, and arduous hours of herding in the sun and the similarly lonely life of the comparatively small camps in the evening. However, it is most important to note that only a fraction of the youths are careless in their herding duties (because of unauthorized visits to markets)— although to hear elders speak of herd-boys one might erroneously believe that practically all of them neglected their tasks. The important point in the new pattern of father–son relationships is that, while only a small percentage of boys leave their fathers to work abroad, the fact that they may do so if provoked is itself a sanction of which modern fathers are fully aware. Defection by a son (especially an only son) is very serious for, as we have seen, the basic economic unit is small and each of its working members is vitally necessary to the whole. Furthermore, a man (like his wife) is entirely dependent on his son in old age.

The reactions of household heads to their problem *vis-à-vis* their sons vary. Not all household heads are equally astute in assessing the reality of the social change, nor are they equally inclined to depart from traditional behaviour. However, through discussions in markets those who have been successful in dealing with their sons informally and often unconsciously instruct those who have greater difficulty. Similarly, among youths, also in the markets, there are exchanges of points of view, one important result of which is that those who do not 'fear' their fathers influence those who do. In this way changing attitudes are diffused through the community. By the same channel youths learn, from those who have travelled, of the possibility of employment as shepherds in Bornu and other areas of Western Sudan, as well as wage labour which appears to be centred mostly in Ghana and Southern Nigeria.[1]

---

[1] The problem of Fulɓe labour migration I consider here only in the aspect of its influence on family discipline. By no means all of these migrations are, of course, the result of a domestic crisis. Some of them are made for the sake of adventure, but they are also an important means whereby money can be obtained to buy more cattle. Still others migrate because of 'shame' (incest, adultery, impotence, &c.) or as fugitives from justice, for example, homicide. A smaller proportion are women who are prostitutes. Informants say that because of their non-negroid features Fulɓe women appeal to the gallants of the south. Absence of migrants is often concealed since their kin tend to feel some embarrassment on the subject of their departure.

The traditional system of enforced obedience (through beating) is losing its effectiveness. There are various new techniques by which men try to win the affection, co-operation, and support of their sons. It was observed, for example, that some herd-owners placed themselves on a herding roster with their sons in order that the latter might have enough free time to enjoy a modicum of social life. In other cases household heads were seen to appeal to the sense of duty of recalcitrant sons, that is, by frequently reminding them that a Pullo who observes 'correct' conduct will always herd for his father. Yet another technique is for men to cajole their sons— to flatter them by telling them how well they have herded and also how much they (the fathers) have appreciated their co-operation.

The various methods by which a man secures the co-operation of his son result in the reduction of the social distance or reserve between the two generations. The fact too that homesteads exist either in isolation or in very small clusters—and without slave labour—means that father and son are obliged to come into more frequent and closer contact than in the past, and this also reduces the status distance between them.

It must not be assumed, however, that the restiveness of youths is due entirely to modern changes, for in part it is to be seen as an anticipation of an adult role of superordination within their own households and the desire to be free of the role of subordination in the household of their fathers. It should be noted that, in those families in which there are several brothers, the elder brothers give early expression to their desire to dominate by exercising authority over their younger brothers. In accepted social usages an elder brother is allowed to strike a younger brother, but the latter is not permitted to retaliate.[1]

Now herd-owners, having once been youths themselves, are well aware of the fact that the only really effective way in which to forestall frustration in a son is to make it clear to him that cattle are available for his marriage. This being so it is clear that the father–son conflict is least acute when there are enough cattle for the needs of the son when the time comes for him to marry. If a man is not able to marry at approximately the same time as his age-fellows he will feel inferior in their company and, owing to the progressive

---

[1] I have seen boys of 3 or 4 years of age strike an elder brother and they were told, with some emphasis (accompanied with a slap), that this would not be tolerated. By the time a lad is 6 or 7 he has accepted the fact without question.

reduction of their community of interests, he cannot fully enjoy their companionship. A man who is old enough to be married, but who is as yet unmarried, is further frustrated since, in his view, his future is being jeopardized; late marriage means small families and delay in gaining a self-sufficient household.

When a son is old enough to get married, or is approaching that age, the tension between him and his father is, potentially, at its greatest. This tension centres about the family herd, for now a son begins to compete with his father for the use of cattle, and ultimately it is the supply of cattle which places a limit on the number of women married by the men of a family. To a father also, as a household head, the marriage of his son marks the beginning of a decline in his own ascendency in his household and foreshadows his future replacement by his son. Whether or not a marked conflict between father and son arises at this stage of family development depends upon various other circumstances of the family. Some of the main principles in this connexion can best be illustrated by an actual field example.[1]

Abdu is a household head of 45 years of age, he has one wife, aged 36, and they have a son Juli (unmarried), 19 years of age. Since Juli has no brothers he has been obliged to herd every day for a number of years; this is so because his father, who is in good health, has made no attempt to give him a break from his herding duties.

Now Abdu has openly admitted, both to myself and his camp fellows, that even though he feels he does not have enough cattle (i.e. about 25) he was trying to find a suitable second wife. He has not expressed any intention to divorce his first wife and this would be unlikely since she bore his son Juli.

Juli has (typically) felt that he has been unfairly treated in that he was one who had to herd every day (*nanganaajo*), but this he tolerated until he learned that his father was about to remarry, which would delay his own marriage. He regarded the proposed action of his father as unjust and it was only a matter of time until he told his father that he would no longer herd. Accordingly, he left home without giving any indication as to the time at which he expected to return.

This case history illustrates several points. Additional information (not cited) shows that relations between Abdu and Juli had not

---

[1] For this, as for other case histories cited in the report, I have used fictitious names. As a condition of receiving much of my data I made it clear to the informants that I would never share the content of their 'secrets' in such a way as to make their identification possible.

been congenial for a number of years and that Abdu lacked confidence and trust in his son. Unlike those of his camp fellows who
were in similar circumstances (in having but one herd-boy), Abdu
did not make any effort to relieve Juli of the monotony of herding.
Excessive herding on the part of Juli seems to have been the main
factor which brought a strain in their relationship in the first instance. But it seems likely that Juli would have continued to herd
for his father if the latter had arranged for him to marry at that
time or in the near future. The son interpreted his father's intention to marry as an action deliberately planned to delay his own
marriage. At the same time, in planning to take a second wife,
Abdu hoped to have sons on whom he might depend in future
years. The desire for more sons might be interpreted as a lack of
confidence in Juli, although this point could not be checked since
it would be indiscreet to ask such a question. For some reason (not
discovered) his wife stopped bearing children after the birth of Juli.

The main point which the case history illustrates is that with
only 25 cattle it would not be possible both for Abdu to take a
second wife and for Juli to marry. Not only would it be difficult to
maintain three wives and two husbands from the existing herd,
but also the initial expense of Juli's marriage (his first) would be
considerable.

It should be noted also that Juli would object to the marriage of
his father 'because of his mother'. Women, especially those who
have not yet reached the menopause, object to their husbands'
taking additional wives and this attitude is transmitted through
the mother to her children.[1] In addition, if Abdu did marry again
and his second wife bore him sons, they would each, legally, have a
share in Abdu's estate equal to the share inherited by Juli. Dividing

---

[1] We have noted that an individual has a much stronger affection for his
mother than for his father. The father is 'liked'—and this is explicitly stated
—because it is through him that cattle are received and, because of the father's
marriage, legitimacy of birth. But a child can never be sure if his pater is his
genitor, 'perhaps the womb was impregnated on the grass (in adultery, not on
the conjugal bed) who knows!' (*kiila reedu nder geene nangete, moye andi!*). On
the other hand, there is never a doubt as to who is the biological mother. To her
affection and gratitude should be felt because she carried the child during its
gestation, withstood the pain of child-birth, gave suck, cleaned and tended
it during its early years. Structurally too, the fact is that a mother and her
young children as legal minors have a sense of solidarity *vis-à-vis* the husband
and father. In the vernacular the different affections towards the parents are
expressed succinctly—towards the mother, *yidde so sei* ('true love') and towards
the father, *yidde dole* ('love of necessity' or 'force').

the estate among half-brothers is not liked in any circumstances, but in this case Juli would be especially averse from the division since for so many years he had been obliged to do all the herding.

When Juli left the household of his father, the attitude of Abdu's age-fellows within the camp was that Juli was right in taking the action he did—although they felt that it was unfortunate. If they had felt Juli was in the wrong they would certainly have said so. The age-mates of Juli would make no comment to the observer, presumably because they thought that he (being of the generation of Abdu and hence their 'father') might be in sympathy with Abdu. The concensus among married men was that Abdu should have been content to remain with one wife until such time as his son married. In general, however, most people felt that the breach was the affair of the father and son alone, which is an attitude in keeping with what we have stressed previously—the independence of the household. If Juli had been under 14 or 15 years of age it is almost certain that an effort would have been made to bring him back. No such action was planned in this case.

If we compare the household of Abdu with similar households (i.e. those with one son) it is clear that if he had had a larger herd, or if he had taken steps to see that his son got more rest, then an open breach might have been averted. In some other households in which there was but one son, it was observed that the father–son relationships were very congenial. In such households the fathers realized that they depended heavily on their sons and did not take their support for granted. For example, in one household, it was noted that the herd-owner had for the past five years hired a herd-boy in order to allow more leisure time for his only son.

In general only sons have strenuous, monotonous, and respon-sible work commitments, but often they cheerfully undertake these in the knowledge that on the death of the father the only son will inherit the total estate. A further fact of interest, discovered in an analysis of marriage case histories, is that only sons tend to marry early. This is linked to the fact that there is little competition for the family herd. It may also be seen as a father's attempt to forestall restiveness (which he can ill afford) in an only son. And a father who himself is deficient in sons desires to facilitate the founding of a family by his son.

A further observation, in the case of Abdu and Juli, should be noted. That is, if Abdu had been older (and hence less interested in remarriage) or Juli younger, or both, then the relations between them might have been more amiable since marriage would not then be a competitive issue involving conflicting demands on a herd of modest size. So long as a boy is under the age of 15 years the age of his father is, as we have seen, of little sociological significance—in the present context.[1] But when a son is old enough to get married, as Juli was, then competition can be an active issue.

In general, men who have but one son feel unfortunate because in these circumstances household management is precarious. Sickness or injury, for instance, of an only son reduces the freedom of the household head, for even if he has a younger daughter (who in any case goes to live with her husband at 15 years of age) it is only rarely that she will be asked to herd. Apart from the fact that herding is not traditionally regarded as the work of girls and women, they are not skilful and hence do not herd except when grazing conditions are most favourable. So if for any reason an only son cannot take the cattle to pasture, then this must be done by the household head.

Now it must be repeated that herding is an extremely wearisome task, by any standard, when considered for a day only, but its drudgery derives from the fact that it must be done by someone every day of the year, and most nights, for a shorter or longer period, throughout the lifetime of each household. This is a feature of pastoral labour which must be stressed, for it stands in marked contrast to the labour requirements of sedentary peoples—the Hausa, for example—who work strenuously when clearing, cultivating, and harvesting have to be done, but during other periods in the year, have abundant leisure, while necessary tasks such as house repair can be performed according to a more or less flexible schedule. The fact that cattle must be tended every day gives urgency to a cattle-owner's herding requirements. The ideal is for a man to have a series of sons so that, as the more senior begin to mature and feel exempt from daily herding, they may be replaced by younger sons who will not question the authority of their father but will tend the cattle as they are instructed.

[1] A point of interest, but one which I do not develop here, is the fact that the age difference between father and son is of great importance in child-rearing. Where the age difference is great, fathers tend to be indulgent. This is doubtless due in part to the fact that sexual jealousy and competition are comparatively slight. It may also be seen as a partial assimilation to alternate generation behaviour in which relations are relaxed.

It was found that, however many sons a man had, he always wanted more,[1] but, of course, the desire is not so strong as that of a man without sons. The possibility of the household population outstripping the increase in the size of the herd is not considered. It is believed that with good luck a herd will increase sufficiently rapidly to meet the requirements of an expanding family. The ideal is to increase the size of one's family and one's herd as much and as quickly as possible. In this there is always a sense of urgency; fertility, both human and bovine, is a 'blessing' and a great practical asset and full advantage should be taken of it. If there are many sons and but a modest herd the marriage of some or all of the sons may be delayed, but always, it is felt, there will be a way, for the same God who provided the sons will provide means for their sustenance. Theoretically this is guaranteed by the greater efficiency of a larger herding force, the fact that sons are available for farming on a rather large scale and that 'surplus' sons may bring in additional income either by herding sheep or in wage-labour. There is thus a tendency in a household for a balance to be reached between the size of the household and the size of the herd. If there are many sons the cattle are attended efficiently and the herd should increase—and the sons may also increase the household income by farming and from labour abroad.

It has been said that only sons marry early, and the reasons for this have been noted. Now among a group of sons the senior son or sons will bear a delay in marriage with some equanimity. This is because, as his junior brothers come of herding age, the duties of the senior brother grow progressively lighter. For, in the Fulɓe view, most of the herding should be done by the junior brothers. In consequence of his greater experience a senior son begins to relieve his father of tasks requiring more judgement (e.g. gathering information on possible future grazing sites) and responsibility. In sharing responsibility with his father, a son who has junior brothers acts as a kind of personal assistant to his father—

---

[1] Men, in particular, stress the economic value of bearing sons. For example, a man of about 50 years of age was once describing his utopian concept of heaven. He mentioned that there would be an abundance of good food and the finest clothing, that there would be no illness, that everyone would have the finest white skin, and so forth. When he mentioned the beautiful women which are promised to the faithful I interjected, 'Then the Fulɓe will be able to have many children?' He replied, 'No, why will we want children? All the work will be done by the servants of Allah.'

a position which is more gratifying and less frustrating than that of an only son. His desire to dominate is given expression as he commands the obedience of his junior brothers. They, in their turn, should show a degree of affection for him—but this is always tempered with deference. Age, as a principal of social organization, is as important within, as it is between, the generations.[1]

The amount of responsibility carried by a senior son varies enormously in the different households. Owing to age and infirmity some fathers are forced to give almost complete responsibility to their senior sons. Other fathers, who are comparatively young and in good health, assign tasks to a senior son according to proven ability, but tend always to maintain a degree of supervision. As a rule, however, whatever his responsibility, a senior son has considerably more free time than his junior brothers. And leisure time is valued in its own right, since considerable status attaches to the individual who is free to associate with his fellows in the markets and thus gain knowledge of the affairs of his community. If his marriage is delayed this is not a matter of acute anxiety (as in the case of an only son) since he knows that his younger brothers will herd for him until he has sons and they have come of herding age.

Now if any man is content it is the man who has several sons, for he is assured that even if there is a domestic crisis, such as the death or defection of a son, the efficiency of the household will continue relatively unimpaired. As he grows older his consideration of the future demands on the herd by unmarried sons restrains his desire to marry additional wives. Adult sons are very critical of their father if he marries a young wife. They have less objection to his marrying an older woman, whom they regard merely as a help-mate for their ageing mother and not as a woman with whom he will have regular sexual relations with the likelihood of her bearing children. Indeed, it is felt that if an old man marries a young wife she, being sexually frustrated, will engage in prostitution—'if an old man marries a young woman she will "enter" into prostitution' (*kul naiejo na howai suka karawanchi na natai*). Such a

---

[1] The importance of age within the generation is expressed linguistically. Senior siblings are *mauniraaɓe* (s. *maunirao*) and junior siblings are *miniraaɓe* (s. *minirao*). If required by context a further term is added to denote the sex, i.e. *debbo* ('female', pl. *reuɓe*) and *gorko* ('male', pl. *worɓe*). When half-siblingship is indicated it is done descriptively so as to make known the actual relationship (*ɓiɓɓe baba*, 'children of a father' and *ɓiɓɓe inna*, 'children of a mother').

marriage may be referred to as *kogal suuno*—'marriage of lust'. Analytically, the aversion from the *kogal suuno* is based on several factors of which the most important are:

1. Young men dislike competition from men of the parental generation for the hand of a potential wife, for one must show deference to the members of the parental generation, which means that an old and a young man do not compete on equal terms.

2. There is an implicit feeling that a husband and wife should be of the same generation. When there is a generation difference there is a conflict arising from the fact that, according to accepted social usages, they should behave towards one another as father and daughter, but because of their marriage they behave as husband and wife.

3. The marriage of an old man to a young woman may be viewed as an attempt on the part of the old man to prolong his control over the cattle. Young men, as sons, are averse from any action which tends to delay their obtaining independent status.

The marriage of an elderly man to a young woman arouses a minimum of public disapproval when the elderly man is comparatively wealthy or has no living sons. His position in either case is atypical and he is allowed, in public opinion, a degree of latitude in adjusting to his circumstances. But if he has adult sons he should put their needs before his own desires and apportion them cattle successively as they marry.

While it does, of course, occur that elderly men marry in *kogal suuno* even when they have adult sons, there is a practical advantage, when cattle are limited, in allowing the sons to have prior claim to the cattle for their marriages. A man who has married (but dependent) sons as his labour force can deploy them with more flexibility and efficiency than he can adult sons who are unmarried. For example, one son and his wife may stay at or near the farm while the other son, also with his wife, tends the cattle at some distance at a more favourable grazing site. Only under short-term conditions of necessity or duress will most herdsmen tolerate, with equanimity, living apart from a housewife (or mother) from whom they can obtain prepared food.

The practical advantage of having married sons is illustrated by a field example. It is convenient also to show other general aspects of the father–son and brother relationships.

This is the case of Donya, aged 64 (1954), of the Jagadanko'en clan. He had one wife who died at the age of 47 in October 1953. Until June 1954, when the inquiry ended, he had not remarried. He has three married sons, Momon, Sidiiku, and Barti, aged 25, 23, and 18 years respectively, none of whom had children.

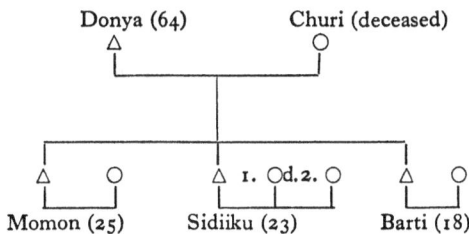

Donya (64)   Churi (deceased)

Momon (25)   Sidiiku (23)   Barti (18)

Since the death of his wife Donya has vaguely expressed the desire to remarry, but it is not a matter which he regards as urgent.

Donya is a very proud father and he has often expressed his pleasure (to Fulɓe as well as to the observer) in his sons. He comments that today 'most' (an exaggeration) youths do not attend to their work, but his sons scrupulously looked after their mother until her death.

Each of the sons married in the order of their birth. Sidiiku has divorced his first wife. She expressed a desire to marry elsewhere so he gave her a divorce. He has since remarried.

Momon and Sidiiku do the farm work each year while Barti, along with Donya, takes the cattle to the wet-season area which is about 40 miles from the farm. The farm labour—from seeding to harvest—took 37 days (1953), or 74 man-days. During the wet season Momon and Sidiiku make short visits to 'see the cattle', but they return to do the periodic weeding and the harvesting.

Whenever possible Donya makes visits to the fields when the sons are working to observe their progress. After greeting them politely he was heard to compliment them by saying, 'you have done well' or, 'you have worked hard'. He was also heard giving them instructions in a quiet manner; for instance, he once told them that they should be more thorough in their weeding and remove weeds which were growing near the fresh corn shoots.

As to the possibility of Donya remarrying, this appears to be unlikely at present, for so long as he has good health he prefers to supervise both the farming and the herding, and at both of these locations he is free to obtain food from his daughters-in-law. However, it is likely that Donya will marry when he grows feeble, for otherwise he would be an encumbrance to his sons who must maintain their mobility. It may be stated with some assurance that when he is too old to endure the hardship of 'following the cattle' he will live permanently in the Haaɓe village nearest the farm (so as to be near the supply of corn). At this time he will find it necessary to marry in order to have a woman to look after him.

The relations among Donya's three sons are most amicable. Momon and Sidiiku, apart from working side by side in farming, spend much of their free time together. They have both expressed affection for Barti and one of them herds for him about one day a week—except, of course, in the wet-season when the herd is far off and Barti must herd every day.

With regard to the pleasant relations with his sons Donya gave no explanation—he only said 'they like me' (*ɓe ngiddi um*).

The total number of cattle possessed by this group was 50 beasts (plus or minus 5).

This case illustrates a point already mentioned (p. 126); the early marriage of the sons has facilitated their seasonal dispersal— Barti living with his wife tending the cattle in the wet season, while his brothers, also with their wives, do the farming.

This is an instance where the process of household development has taken place without signs of acute conflict or tension— so far. Donya was one of the most intelligent informants found and it was obvious that he applied his intelligence in handling his sons.[1] He remained monogamous throughout his lifetime and used the cattle reserve for the marriage of his sons. He was fortunate in having enough cattle to allow them to marry early, thus forestalling their frustration and hostility. A more selfish or less perceptive father might well have used the reserve of cattle for himself to marry, thus delaying the marriage of his sons and alienating their affections. It is in this light that we can interpret his statement 'they like me'.

As we have seen in the case history, the delay in Donya's remarriage was probably deliberate, but there are one or two additional facts which should be noted. For example, it was clear from observation during his wife's lifetime that he did have a more than usually strong affection for his wife. It may be, in part, that out of grief over the loss of his wife he delayed remarriage, both for his own sake and to maintain the respect of his children. Information of this kind is hard to get directly since Fulɓe prefer to bear their

---

[1] No doubt some of the indulgence shown by Donya can be explained in terms of the age difference between him and his sons: he is 39 years older than his eldest son. Donya was of the age group of the classificatory grandfathers of his sons. Moreover, because he was almost 60 years of age when his senior son married, there could have been little sexual competition between them.

sorrow in silence. Delays 'because of grief' have been recorded in other marriages. However, he was in a position to delay remarriage for, as we have seen, he could obtain food from his daughters-in-law. Being thus obliged to live with his sons he remained in close contact with them and would, therefore, be able to reconcile differences among them. If, on the other hand, he were to re-marry, his sons might well suggest that he should live in the nearby Haaɓe village (nearby, that is, for only part of the year) and there he would not be aware of the possible conflicts among his sons. The presence of even an aged father among his sons seems to restrain conflicts among them.

The friendly and co-operative relations among the sons has a structural basis in the fact that they had as yet no sons, so that only with extreme difficulty would they be able to maintain spatially separated households. If they did so it would probably mean that they would have to abandon farming or would require wage labour which would have to be paid from the sale of stock. Wider observation has made it clear that when a group of herd-owners are camped together there are rarely overt signs of frustration and hostility; and it was also learnt that the Fulɓe are past masters at suppressing these tendencies so long as it is to their mutual advantage to remain together.

With regard to the three sons it should be noted that the stage at which the conflict potential is greatest had not yet been reached. So long as they do not have children they are economically dependent upon each other and, also because they have no children, their interests are still centred in their natal family—their father and each other. With the arrival of children their field of interest gradually shifts to their family of procreation, upon whose loyalty, devotion, and affection their future depends. So long as Donya lives, however, it is unlikely that his sons will feel complete freedom of individual decision and, for the sake of their father, they would attempt to suppress latent conflicts which might arise among them. As a rule, when a man grows old he attempts more and more to exert moral influence,[1] albeit without effective

---

[1] I use the word 'influence' advisedly, rather than 'authority' because authority presupposes the control of sanctions. An old man (*naiejo*) who has stopped 'following' cattle does not, owing to his declining health and approaching senility, occupy an important position of status, for in the Fulɓe view 'an old man and a four-year-old are both the same' (in 'importance') (*naiejo i naiijo ɓe fuh ɓe go'o*). An old man having given his cattle to his sons has given up *the* sanction from

sanctions, while his sons progressively replace him in domestic authority.

The structural and spatial separation of sons as they severally establish individual households is reluctantly recognized by the Fulɓe as inevitable, but their theories as to the way in which this should come about are seen to vary. Some herdsmen, being loath to accept the reality of the separation of sons, hold that they should remain together as long as possible. Elderly men, in particular, strongly stress the ideal of sibling solidarity and in so doing attempt to restrain inherent (or incipient) fissiparous tendencies. Some herd-owners say that it is better if each son establishes, if possible, his own independent and spatially separated household during the lifetime of the father—the separation should be deliberate, or not discouraged.

This ambivalent attitude towards the formation of new households may be viewed, analytically, as a reflection of the various circumstances in which the informants have been conditioned. But it is also an aspect of the uneven process of social change, which is not equally perceived by all. Those informants who prefer that sons remain together indefinitely are attempting to perpetuate what they believe to have been the traditional—and hence the 'correct' system. On the other hand, herdsmen who are not averse from the early separation of their sons more clearly recognize the present-day structural and ecological reality and have, in some measure, adjusted their attitudes to it. Those who feel that fissiparous tendencies should not be inhibited hold that sons who feel at liberty to separate will also feel free to call upon each other for co-operation should the need arise, and such sons are likely to maintain amicable relations throughout their lifetime. While each grown man may desire to assert his independence, it is also considered advisable to be on good terms with as many other household heads as possible, so that should the need for co-operation arise in the future, the channels will be open. In their own words; 'who knows what will come to pass tomorrow?' (i.e. 'in the future', *moye andi ko wontiri jaango?*).

In order to illustrate the father–son and brother relationship in

which previously all his authority derived. Old and cattleless he expresses himself in the only way open to him—by making value judgements and offering moral advice. According to the varying sense of duty and 'conscience' of his sons he gets a hearing.

another context a further case history is cited in which the circumstances differ from the cases cited above. In this case the father is older, he has had more sons (who were born of two wives), some of whom are in a position to head autonomous households.

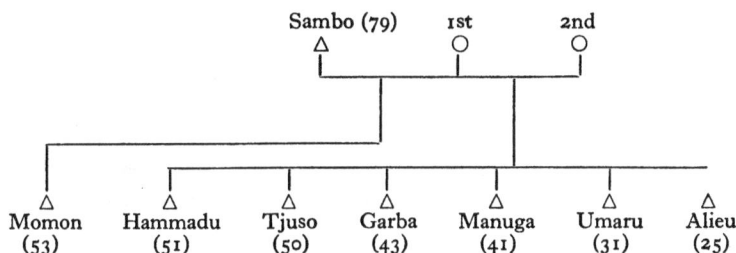

Sambo, who is 79 years of age, came to his present area, with his second wife and children, about 40 years ago. He left his natal home, which is 15 miles from Sokoto, in order that he might seek out better pastures. At present he lives in a permanent compound in village 'X' which is about 100 miles south-west of his original home.

Sambo has seven living sons. The senior son, Momon, is the only living son of his father's first wife who died in the fifth year of her marriage. The remaining sons were borne by Sambo's second wife. Five of the sons, Momon, Hammadu, Tjuso, Garba, and Manuga have at least one son over the age of 7 years. Umaru's eldest son is 4 years of age and Alieu, although he was married for one year, is now divorced and has no children.

The four senior sons (Momon, Hammadu, Tjuso, and Garba) each had spatially separated and economically self-sufficient households. Although Tjuso has one son of herding age he has a hired herd-boy to assist the son. Hammadu still lives at the natal home of his father near Sokoto and he visits his father, mother, and brothers only once every two or three years.

Although the four elder brothers are economically self-sufficient there is still intensive economic co-operation among the three younger brothers. Both Umaru and Alieu keep their cattle with their next most senior brother Manuga, whose two sons (aged 11 and 8 years) do the herding. Alieu does the farm labour required for the support of his father and mother and when he has free time Alieu helps Manuga with night herding. Umaru is with a herd of sheep near Dogonduchi in the French Niger. The sheep are owned jointly by the three younger brothers.[1]

---

[1] Most Gwandu Fulɓe do not own sheep, but a small proportion may have from 2 to 10 or more which are herded with the household cattle. If, however, as

Sambo says that when he first came to the present area he had 50 cattle. Today the senior brothers have about 50 cattle each while the younger brothers, who form the economic unit described above, have from 25 to 40 cattle each. The younger brothers, severally, have sufficient cattle to maintain economically self-sufficient households, but their shortage of sons of herding age inhibits any tendency for them to establish autonomous households.

The attitude of Sambo towards the separation of his senior sons is one of marked concern. Without his view being solicited he expressed much disappointment over their separating and he would prefer them to stay together. He holds that his senior sons have established separate households because they do not have an affection for each other such as they should have.

The 'reasons' given by Sambo's sons for their dispersal are various. Some of them say that they can better meet the pasturing needs of their cattle if the herds are separated and among Sambo's sons there are differences of view as to which is the best area to graze during a given season. Some of the sons also say that they are obliged to separate since their wives do not get on together. But the most realistic reason given by one of the sons was that every man likes to command his own affairs, a factor which is precluded, to some extent, when a man is in co-residence with a senior brother.[1]

If Sambo is disturbed by the fact that his sons do not remain together he is more upset by the fact that they do not appear to be fond of him and they do not accord him the respect which he considers to be his due. On one occasion Tjuso told his father to make a calf-rope. Sambo complained that he was too old and not well enough to do the work. After Tjuso insisted on the old man doing the task Sambo began—protesting,

happens, the sheep herd increases to more than say 30 animals Fulɓe consider it practical, if domestic manpower permits, to herd the sheep separately. In the wet season, in particular, sheep do not thrive well in the pastoral conditions favourable to cattle. Sheep mortality is high if they are exposed to heavy rainfall and dew and this is why the ideal wet-season grazing zone for sheep is farther north than it is for cattle.

[1] I observed one case in which a divorced man without children returned with his cattle to live with his younger brother. The elder brother, in this instance, was dependent on his younger brother (through the latter's wife) for prepared food. To compensate his younger brother the elder brother herded both his own cattle and those of his younger brother each day—the younger brother would, of course, do the bulk of the herding if both brothers were married and living together on a permanent, or quasi-permanent, basis. Since this case is of some interest it is unfortunate that I was not able to observe it for a longer period. However, it may be stated with some assurance that it would not be long until the elder brother remarried and at that time he would re-establish an independent household or, if he remained with his younger brother, the latter would do most of the herding.

meanwhile, that Tjuso was trying to kill him. At this point Tjuso, not taking his father's comment seriously, laughed heartily.

Sambo has, in some measure, come to expect that his elder sons will pay little attention to his wishes; but he is disappointed with Alieu who, as the youngest son, should still heed his father's wishes. In comparison with his elder brothers Alieu does show deference to his father despite Sambo's assertion to the contrary. Alieu, being without a wife and family (and hence being regarded socially as a minor), devotes much of his time to the care of his father. It should be noted, as a general observation, that children who are born late in the reproductive cycle of their parents are indulged by the latter. This is in contradistinction to the relatively harsher treatment given to children who are born when the parents are still young.

Recently Sambo was very pleased because Garba gave him an expensive gown. But a friend of Garba's brother Alieu mentioned that the other brothers were annoyed since they felt that Garba was attempting to gain the favour of the father. Although Sambo says that he has given all his cattle to his sons, the occurrence of jealousy, in this instance, suggests that Sambo still holds some animals of his original herd.

Further, it should be noted that the sons were very annoyed with their father because, when he was 68 years old, he married a comparatively young woman. This woman bore a daughter several years ago. The attitude of the sons was that the father, as an old man, should have confined his marital interests to their mother. For old people 'the afterlife is near' and they should be content to obtain food and shelter, they should not be interested in contracting further marriages, and in the household affairs of their sons they should be unobtrusive.

But whatever the attitude of the sons to their father they frequently visit his compound when their cattle are grazed in the vicinity of village 'X'. To the experienced observer it is quite obvious that Momon is a half-brother. He does not visit Sambo as often as his younger half-brothers do and when he does visit he tries to select a time when he knows that his half-brothers will not be present. If Momon is present during a visit of his younger half-brothers he often sits apart from them; indeed, before I became aware of the genealogy of this group, I had the impression that Momon was a friend or a remote kinsman.[1] In the

---

[1] Antipathy between half-siblings arises in part through early conditioning by the respective mothers of half-siblings. A co-wife makes no attempt to conceal from her children, as she may from her husband, the animosity which she may feel towards a co-wife. Young children, being strongly influenced by their mother, extend their attitude of hostility towards their half-siblings. However, Fulße hold, and this is empirically confirmed, that relations between half-siblings are more amiable in small compound families. Analytically this is linked to the necessary suppression of inherent conflicts in the interest of intra-familial

conversations of the sons of Sambo's second wife there is only occasional reference to the elder half-brother.

Informants from outside the group mention that it is only because of a sense of duty that Sambo's sons continue to visit him. The same informants say that once the father (and mother) have died the sons will separate permanently, but so long as the father is living they feel obliged to feign a degree of affection for each other so that they will not upset the father unduly. The position with regard to the sentiments between brothers was perhaps overstated by one informant when he said: 'If you were to go to a Pullo and say, "here is a cow and here is your brother, which shall I kill?" the Pullo would answer, "kill my brother".'

This case history has been selected in order to show the final stage of household development. Sambo is now so old that, apart from serving, functionally, as a symbol of the common origin of his sons, he is no longer socially significant. But despite his sincere complaints that his sons do not care for him Sambo is a proud father, for he has fulfilled an important ideal in the society—he has begotten many sons and each of them has sufficient cattle for his needs. From Sambo's original herd of 50 cattle there are now something like 250 to 300 animals. In respect of this success he is pleased, but he does not openly express his pleasure. However, since for so many years he had been in active command of a household—and enjoyed the attendant authority—he does not easily adjust himself to his 'retirement'. So far as his sons are concerned they feel obliged only to provide him with his basic subsistence needs (even this they find irksome) and to accord him a modicum of respect. But they are mainly concerned to care for their respective households and herds and to try to increase both, even as their father did. With this ambition before them, doting on their father is a waste of time.

Further mention of Sambo and his sons will be made below in the summary of this section.

General Analysis and Summary

The structure of the household is best perceived if the society is visualized as a series of households each of which is, at a given moment, at a specific level in its development. The interests, ambitions, roles, and status of the members of a household vary

co-operation. The above case gives structural provision for a maximum expression of hostility between the half-siblings since Sambo's second wife bore so many sons that co-operation outside the full sibling group is not necessary.

according to the level of development of that household; so also, therefore, must the nature of the relationships among the members change in time. Some of the implications of this are noted below.

A boy begins to be economically productive at 7 years of age. Until he is 14 or 15 he is under the absolute authority of his father. It is only during this interval that the Fulɓe ideal of discipline-respect between father and son is followed to the letter. For when a boy is about 15 years of age he can, for the first time, effectively withdraw his herding co-operation. This is the beginning of the decline of the father's authority.

Paternal authority is further reduced when a son reaches 18 years of age and upwards, marries, and receives his own cattle from his father's herd. However, a man who has a number of sons can prolong his authority, for so long as he has minor sons he maintains a reserve of cattle for their future marriages and, until they found their own households, these cattle are tended by them under their father's direction. It can be seen, therefore, that a household head has a practical motive (in addition to those noted above) for desiring a number of sons. For it is through the future claims of young and unmarried sons (on cattle which must be held in reserve) that a father resists the demands of his married sons.

A man entirely loses authority over his son when the latter, in his turn, has a son of herding age. A man's right to command a labour force is limited to his younger brothers (when the father is absent, incapable, or dead) and his sons. A man exercises no authority over his grandson; this would be incongruent with social usages, for between alternate generations relations are free and easy and there is also moderate joking.[1] This point was checked quantitatively and it was found that in 100 households there was no instance in which a herd-boy came under the authority of his grandfather.

When a man's senior son (or sons) establishes a self-sufficient household the father may still exercise authority over his junior

[1] The special character of the grandparent–grandchild (real and classificatory) relationship is referred to by the vernacular term *tolla*. It is distinguished conceptually and terminologically from the joking relationship which obtains between cross-cousins (*dendá*, also *dendiraagu*). A grandfather may scold or slap his very young grandchildren for boisterous behaviour, for example, in the precincts of the shelters—but he does not have a voice in organizing the activities of herd-boys. Grandparents, in joking, refer to their grandchildren as slaves. This may be interpreted as an ironical allusion to their lack of authority over them.

sons until such time as they, severally, have sons to maintain their own households. Should a man die before his sons are married, then the senior son will automatically succeed to the household headship occupied by his father. Secession from this household will take place by stages as each of the men have sons able to tend their cattle. The principle is illustrated in the case of Sambo's sons, for although Sambo is still alive he can be regarded as socially dead. Today the younger sons continue to co-operate since they (with the exception of Manuga) do not have sons of sufficient age for them to maintain independent households. This case also shows that the inclination to co-operate among male siblings is greatest when the age difference between them is comparatively small. Not only do they have a similar field of interests, but also the principle of seniority, which is important in the sibling group, is less pronounced (and hence less irksome to a younger brother) when there is little age difference between the siblings. Herdsmen say that respect and deference should be shown to one's seniors because they have lived longer and thus should have greater wisdom (*'andal*). But while a Pullo feels that this attitude is 'right', he acts accordingly only so long as it is necessary. He looks forward to the time when he will command his own household and will be his own master.

It is by having a son of herding age that a man finally gains complete independence from his father (or senior brother). This is guaranteed by the pastoral tradition that a son must herd the cattle of his father (or senior brother) and is not obliged to herd other cattle. But the same son who gave his father independence gradually usurps his father's authority as he grows older. The threat of a son's withdrawing herding co-operation is the only sanction, but a powerful one, which he can apply against his father; first to get considerate treatment and then to receive cattle. Finally, with his cattle gone through the marriage of his sons, a man spends the last years of his life as he did his first—as a dependant. In his youth, because of his lack of experience, he depended on his father. In his old age, because of his lack of vigour, he depends on his sons.

14

PATTERN OF INHERITANCE

THE system of Fulɓe inheritance today[1] differs in some particulars from the system which is held to have obtained during the 'Time of War'. Moreover, since the area covered in the research is rather wide and includes people who formerly came from an even wider area, it is not to be expected that the system of inheritance will be uniform throughout the region. Nevertheless, there is general agreement that, in the past, when a man died his cattle passed to his senior son who later apportioned them successively to his junior brothers as they reached the appropriate age for marriage. In those days, it is said, only a cow or two was given to the daughters of the deceased—usually when they became established in the households of their husbands. It should also be noted that the brothers of the dead man, especially if his senior son was a minor, took an active part in advising the senior son and arranging his marriage and those of his junior brothers. The structurally important fact is that, in the past, the senior brother occupied an important place in the sibling group since it was he who controlled the distribution of cattle among his junior brothers. This is, in part, why Fulɓe hold that in the past the sibling group was characterized by much solidarity (*sumpo*), for in the sibling group no one would challenge the status of the senior brother.

Today the Fulɓe system of inheritance, strictly speaking, follows neither the 'traditional' system nor the system prescribed by Maliki Law.[2] For various reasons the traditional system holds with considerable force in some households, while a system predominantly in accordance with Maliki obtains in others. The analysis of the functional significance of this range in pattern is not considered here, for it is an extremely involved question which is not germane to the present account. But part of our answer clearly lies in the fact that not all the households are equally influenced by the

[1] I confine the discussion to the inheritance of cattle. To the pastoralists this type of property is by far the most important.

[2] I do not detail the complex inheritance law of Maliki. The reader is referred to F. H. Ruxton, *Maliki Law*, 1916, pp. 373–97.

modern political situation even if they had a similar background in the past.

It is important to mention that the explicit policy of the Native Administration aims to bring the Fulɓe within the sphere of Native Authority jurisdiction as much as possible. Accordingly the Native Authority endeavours to settle pastoral inheritance cases in the District Courts—with, so far, varying degrees of success. The Native Authority argues that, if there is court settlement of inheritance, not only will the courts increase their revenue, but also the number of inheritance disputes among the Fulɓe will be reduced.

Fulɓe are averse, for various reasons, from having questions of inheritance settled by the courts. Most pastoralists are fully aware that, according to Islam, they are obliged to settle inheritance cases in the courts and according to specific rules. However, they are prepared to evade certain of the more irksome obligations of Islam if these conflict too strongly with their personal interests. Certainly Fulɓe are proud to call themselves Mohammedans and they arrogate prestige to themselves on the strength of the support given by some of their ancestors to the Jihad. But pastoralists regard the Native Authority as machinery of the Haaɓe and, by a process of transference, their traditional attitude of hostility towards the Haaɓe is applied to the Native Authority. Since the Native Authority has the backing of the British Administration it is too 'strong' for the Fulɓe, so their best defence is obscurity, for the court is viewed rather as an institution to be feared than as a means whereby a Pullo may receive redress. The herdsmen reluctantly admit that they do not adhere to the high standards of Islam as closely as they should, but this is less reprehensible in them than in the Haaɓe, whose faith in Islam is 'in the mouth only, not in the heart' (*Haaɓe diina maɓɓe nder handuuko woni hanna nder bernde*). It is true, the Fulɓe argue, that according to Maliki Law the inheritors are obliged to forfeit one-tenth of the estate in death duties (Ar. *ushera*) but, they go on, the Haaɓe are corrupt and, since they misappropriate funds in the Islamic state, the Fulɓe are not obliged to contribute to revenue which will be misused. Fulɓe would, they say somewhat piously, gladly pay death duties if the Administration was composed of men of better character (*gikku*) and the revenue was correctly expended.

Other pastoralists argue that inheritance is not a question which concerns the District *Alkali* since it is an 'affair of the household' (*haraka wuro*) and it should correctly be settled by the immediate kin of the deceased.

But whatever the Fulɓe attitude towards the court it is clear that the multiplication of *alkalis* under the Protectorate (ten *alkalis* today for fifteen districts as opposed to one court in the capital during the pre-Protectorate period) has had an influence not only on inheritance custom but also on other aspects of Fulɓe social organization. It is emphatically and explicitly stated that it is wrong for a Pullo to take another Pullo to court—and especially a kinsman or clansman—but the occasional occurrence of this and the possibility of its happening in the future, act as a sanction which influences the pastoralists when they are settling a matter of inheritance. Quite apart from their aversion from paying death duties herdsmen do not favour the Maliki system of inheritance whereby a daughter receives one-half of a son's share. Cattle are traditionally the property of men and any system whereby women acquire animals is regarded with disfavour. There is less objection to the fact that under Maliki Law the principle of primogeniture does not operate, for thus all sons receive an equal inheritance.

Whatever principle of inheritance is applied in practice, only a small proportion of cattle are transmitted by inheritance in each generation. A man, as we have seen, gives cattle to his sons successively as they marry and, if he lives until all his sons have married, he will spend his last years as their dependant. On his death he will have no cattle to pass on to them. If a large herd is inherited it generally means that the late owner had only very young sons or no sons at all. The more usual pattern is that when a man dies he leaves no cattle or only a few beasts. Some informants hold that in order to reduce the number of cattle passed in inheritance a proportion of herd-owners accelerate (in comparison with the past) the distribution of their cattle among their sons and by so doing three things are accomplished:

1. The necessity of paying death duty in the court is avoided.

2. The likelihood of daughters receiving a large share in a court settlement is eliminated.

3. The possibility of disputes among the sons (which are regarded as likely if there is an estate) is avoided.

Even when inheritance is settled without reference to the *alkali's* court there seems to be a growing tendency to settle according to the principles of Maliki Law. For example, an informant once said: 'Today if you do not give your sister her share of the cattle (from her father's estate) her husband will say, "where is your share of the cattle left by your father?" Then will you not be called (by the brother-in-law) before the *alkali*?' Other examples could be cited, but this illustrates the tendency to distribute property in accordance with Maliki Law so as to avoid summons by an *alkali* on the initiative of an aggrieved party. However, the fact that inheritance is not crystallized in a uniform pattern can be illustrated by another example. A Pullo informant said that his elder brother had claimed the ownership of all their father's cattle on the death of the father. He added, 'What can I do? I cannot (for ethical reasons) take my brother before the *alkali*'.

It is clear that the pattern of inheritance has undergone, and is still undergoing, change. But no attempt to establish a detailed cause-effect relationship is made here. It may, however, be suggested that today junior brothers do not remain in a subordinate relationship to their senior brother to the same extent as in the past. It is true that the hiving-off of brothers was primarily inhibited in the past by the fact that the Fulɓe lived in a wider community of much political instability and, for their common defence, were compelled to live in comparatively large-scale units. In contrast, under the present Administration, security is such that younger brothers are free to move off as they wish and, when inheritance is settled according to Maliki principles, their hiving-off is not inhibited by a prior claim on the inheritance by the senior brother. The principal factor militating against the dispersal of brothers today is their shortage of herd-boys, in the early stages of their family, to tend the domestic herd.

15

POLYGYNY

A MAN'S desire to be head of a polygynous household arises, as in other societies, from a number of motives. Some men express satisfaction at having only one wife while others are eager to have two or more. Informants of about 30 years of age and upwards tend to favour having one or two wives, but rarely more. Among themselves men discuss enthusiastically and at length the merits and demerits of monogamous and polygynous households. But such discussions rarely produce accord, since the circumstances of each household and the past experience of each household head differ. Thus, for example, a household head who has aged parents and no sons may feel a pressing need for more than one wife so that he can leave one wife to care for his parents while the other is free to travel with him and his cattle; another man who has a number of sons may feel that it is wiser to have one wife, for in marrying another he may lose the affection of his sons and their mother. In general, it is only rarely that a man will marry more than one wife as a simple and direct bid for higher status. Indeed, both community and household status can be quickly lost by a man who marries more women than he can afford, or who by his marriages delays the marriages of his sons.

Among men in general two of the most important motives for polygynous marriages are the desire to beget many children, sons in particular, and an attempt to increase domestic security. We have seen that it is necessary to have at least one wife in each household. Men frequently say that it is good to have more than one wife so that should one desert, the household head's domestic requirements will still be met. However, as will be seen, women in polygynous households are difficult to manage and a high proportion of informants say that it is better to remain with one contented wife than to risk her leaving because of her husband's second marriage.

A man whose wife is old or infirm may find it necessary to take a second wife to do most of the women's work in the household. When polygynous marriage takes place in order to gain status the husband is often a young man who has more cattle than his age-fellows—usually an only son whose father has died. Older men, if only because they have marriageable sons, tend to be less impulsive in taking additional wives.

Young women in particular are openly hostile to the idea of their husbands' taking second or subsequent wives. Yet since, as has been said, the husband–wife relationship is non-symmetrical, a woman cannot openly protest when her husband plans or effects another marriage. But Fulße women are not at a loss when it comes to contriving domestic sanctions by which to show their objections and to test their husband's affections for them. A husband who plans or has quietly contracted a second marriage may find that his senior wife suddenly becomes sullen and depressed. She may complain that she can get little money from the sale of the dairy produce and that corn is expensive. She may also complain of severe headaches, rheumatism, or an upset stomach, whether real or fictitious, which gives her an excuse to be inefficient in her labour and to refuse sexual union. The combination of these and other sanctions usually provokes an argument which may decide whether the first or second wife will remain with the husband.

Like men in their own sphere most women believe in and, so far as one can tell, a fair proportion of them use social medicine to assuage their jealousy by attempting to nullify the attractions of their competitors and increase their own appeal to their husbands. The general terms for such medicines are *magani*[1] *togu* ('popularity medicine') and *magani worße* ('medicine for men'). Men believe that women have an elaborate knowledge and vocabulary of social medicine which is confined to their own sex. We were not able to get much information from men or women. However, some women say that medicines do exist which prevent a man from achieving an erection with a competing woman, or from being otherwise attracted to her. Some men believe, with enormous disgust, that in order to make themselves irresistibly attractive sexually some women put a small quantity of water, in which they have done their genital ablutions, into the food of their husband.

Between co-wives jealousy is partially counteracted by the strict obligation of a man to treat his wives equally. If, for example, a man

---

[1] *Magani* is a Hausa term for 'medicine' which is much more frequently used than the Fulfulde synonym *lekki*. The Fulfulde term is probably going out of use because a proportion of medicine is acquired from Hausa-speaking Haaße.

gives a cloth or kola-nuts to one wife he must give the same quality and quantity to her co-wife. He must sleep with his wives in turn, one night each. His sleeping partner at night is the wife who prepared his food on the same day. A co-wife is very alert to recognize signs of not being impartially treated and she reacts by applying domestic sanctions, deserting or seeking a divorce in the courts, according to her inclination or the seriousness of her husband's breach of his obligations. Indeed a wife may desert, often on previous instructions from her mother, the moment a co-wife comes to live at the homestead. For women are sceptical about the likelihood of happiness in a polygynous household and say, 'if (in a polygynous household) one woman laughs the other will cry'. They also say 'can a woman be happy when she hears[1] her husband having sexual intercourse with her co-wife?'

But nevertheless a woman who is old and infirm will offer little objection to her husband's taking a second wife for she knows that she cannot fulfil her domestic duties and she may welcome assistance.

Wives are ranked according to the order of their marriages. The senior wife (*wargidaajo*) has little formal authority over a junior wife[2] (*sunkuujo*) although in certain contexts the seniority of the first wife is expressed. For example, a stranger or a friend of an absent household head will address his inquiries to the senior wife, and she, in turn, may direct a junior wife to bring a sleeping mat for the visitor. But food and milk will come from the calabashes of the senior wife. The shelter of the first wife is also a recognized repository for the more valuable personal effects of the household head—his best robe and turban, his sword, saddlery, and so forth. After making a move the household head first erects the shelter of his senior wife and builds the shelters for junior wives in the order of their seniority.

But even though a senior wife has relatively high prestige, she cannot command the economic co-operation of a junior wife.

---

[1] At certain times of the year, as I have noted, Fulɓe do not build shelters. At such times co-wives (one of whom is with her husband) sleep on mats sometimes only about 5 yards apart. But even if there are shelters, construction is so flimsy and they are often so close together that every sound can be overheard. However, husbands are sufficiently discreet to delay sexual activity until they assume that the lone co-wife is asleep.

[2] Terms which indicate rank (*wargidaajo* senior and *sunkuujo* junior) and order of marriage (*arendeejo*—1st, *didabro*—2nd, *tatabro*—3rd, and *naiabo*—4th) are used in reference only.

Each wife has exclusive milking rights in specific cattle and the utensils necessary for all her domestic activities. However, the proximity of the shelters of co-wives makes domestic co-operation between them convenient, should their congenial relations so incline them. But, as a rule, women lack confidence in their ability to remain on good terms with a co-wife for long, and tend to co-operate only in emergencies, at other times maintaining a polite reserve. If the age difference between co-wives is great then the junior wife will show considerable respect for the senior wife because of her age and also because of fear of the influence which the senior wife, through long cohabitation, has over the husband.

Two co-wives agree best when their husband marries a third wife. It is perhaps for this reason that men say that it is difficult to manage a household of three wives.

Both men and women freely admit the latent jealousy and hostility between co-wives. They say that the taboo on co-wives entering each other's shelters, except by mutual consent when there is good will, is a measure to avoid harm, through magical means or poisoning, to each other.[1]

The incidence of polygyny is relatively high because men marry at a later age than women and, also, to a lesser extent, because a proportion of the young men of Gwandu Emirate spend a number of years abroad. Some of them leave the Emirate before they marry and others who were married before they left may, if they stay away for long, be divorced by proxy on the instance of the wife.

In a random sample it was found that 200 men, of all ages, who had marital experiences were married to 278 women—a husband wife ratio of 1 to 1·4. Sixty-seven of the 200 households—33·5 per cent.—were polygynous. There were 6 men (3%) in the sample with previous marital experience but who, at the time of the inquiry, were not married. One hundred and twenty-seven men (63·5%) were monogamous; 55 men (27·5%) had 2 wives; 9 men (4·5%) had 3 wives; 1 man ($\frac{1}{2}$%) had 4 wives; and 2 men (1%) had 5 wives—one more than the legal limit permitted by Islam.

The number of marriages contracted is even greater, of course, than the number of wives actually in households. The 200 men

[1] One 'medicine' which is especially feared is *magani kurchi* ('medicine above the doorway'). It is believed that a hostile wife may place a herbal concoction above the doorway of a co-wife's shelter. The magical properties of the concoction, it is thought, may cause illness, death, or sterility of the victim or loss of the husband's favour.

during their lives had married 480 women, a marriage ratio of 2·4 per head, the highest number of marriages were contracted by a man of about 48 years of age who was arranging his 21st marriage on the day his marriage history was recorded. While marriages to such a large number of women are exceptional another man (age 66) had married 14 times, and 5 or more divorces for one man are quite frequent.

There are reasons to believe that the incidence of polygynous marriage and of divorce has increased in recent years. Our evidence suggests that, for various reasons—the breakdown of the clan organization with its betrothal arrangements, opportunities for men in outside labour, and other factors—the difference in age between spouses at first marriage is increasing. Girls marry at or about the same age as they did in the past, but men marry later. This provides a favourable condition for an increase in polygyny. Since Fulße women are strongly averse from living in polygynous households we might link an increase in divorce and desertion with the increase in polygyny—but there are clearly many other operative factors.

16

THE FAMILY IN ITS WIDER SETTING

BEFORE discussing the family in relation to other families and to the clan, it is necessary to give a general description of the society in terms of the wider Hausa-speaking community. Fulɓe–Haaɓe relations are essentially symbiotic in character and the pastoral system, in particular, cannot be fruitfully discussed without reference to the Haaɓe. It is only possible here to indicate certain of the more important features of the relations between the two ethnic groups; but the importance of the problem is not minimized; it is an extremely complex subject and its detailed treatment is beyond the scope of this report.

Certain effects of social change have been frequently emphasized, but in one important respect the influence of the 'Time of War' still actively dominates social relations; this is in regard to the behaviour between the Fulɓe and the Haaɓe. From the point of view of the pastoralists the earlier servile status of the Haaɓe is not easily forgotten. And in the modern context of conflict over land for pasture on the one hand and for cultivation on the other, the former status difference between them is renewed and perpetuated. The salient feature of the attitudes of the two ethnic groups towards each other is hostility, the intensity of which varies according to circumstances. In their relations with the Haaɓe the herdsmen see themselves as a group who are not only ethnically and culturally distinct (and superior), but who are also occupationally specialized and have a common body of interests and problems. In addition, through their remote kinship with the Torooɓe, the ruling dynasty of Gwandu and Sokoto, the Fulɓe in any neighbourhood claim to be the local *élite*. The unanimously accepted belief of herdsmen is that in culture and intelligence they are superior to the Haaɓe. This idea is supported by a myth which relates how Shehu said that when God created man he made the Fulɓe 'superior' to the Haaɓe. It is also felt that the Haaɓe are jealous of the 'wealth' of the Fulɓe and are determined to destroy it. And one further point is that the Haaɓe feel a 'grudge' (say the pastoralists) towards the Fulɓe for having established their suzerainty in the past.

Systematic inquiry among Haaɓe peasants in Gwandu showed that they, on their part, regard the pastoralists as being fanatically attached to cattle and, in consequence (in Haaɓe logic), having little more 'intelligence' than their animals. That the conflict is in part economic is seen in the fact that the peasants say that the herd-owners will deliberately pasture cattle on crops if they think that they can escape detection. It is important also to note that the Haaɓe contest the claim of the Fulɓe to be local *élites* by asserting that they themselves are today more learned and orthodox in Islam than are the Fulɓe. The argument has, in fact, some substance for almost all the scholars at the Koranic schools are Haaɓe (as are also the students at the 'European' schools). Learning in Mohammedanism is an important item in the acquisition of prestige. But in gaining such learning modern Fulɓe are seriously handicapped, since not only are herd-boys continuously needed in their households but also seasonal movements make regular attendance at school impossible. In contrast the Haaɓe are sedentary and, because their work is seasonal, their youths have leisure time. In the past the position was reversed because routine tasks were done by slaves and the Fulɓe had free time in which to study. But on this point we must be chary of generalizing for in the 'Time of War' (as today) not all Fulɓe were equally interested and instructed in Islam. In so far as reconstruction is possible it may be stated in general that religious observance and learning were greatest among the inhabitants of Gwandu and Sokoto towns and decreased progressively with the spatial distance of village communities from these centres.[1]

These are the more important of the stereotyped attitudes that obtain between the two ethnic groups. But it is more important that certain facts in Fulɓe–Haaɓe political relations be noted. When the Protectorate was established the administrative units of the district and of the village were made, so far as possible, to coincide with the traditional boundaries. The population of a given village obtained

---

[1] It was apparent to me that those Fulɓe whose ancestral home was within say 10 or 20 miles of Sokoto but who are now living in Gwandu Emirate, feel superior to other Fulɓe who traditionally did not move far, for example, from the Niger— an area which is still to some extent regarded as hinterland.

usufructory rights to village-area lands through its Village Head. The Village Head was the link with the District Head and through him with the Emir. Lying at the base of the State organization of the modern Emirate is this clear-cut territorial series, namely: the Emirate, the District, and the Village, and associated with each are the Emir, the District Head, and the Village Head, respectively. For the present we are most interested in discussing certain features of the village community.

The fact that the Fulɓe chose to leave their traditional clan-villages after the British conquest has entirely altered their political status and has placed them in an anomalous position. This is so because the basis of the political organization of the village community is a clearly defined territory—the village area—and the permanent residence of its members. A Village Head gains and maintains his office through the support of the permanent members of his village. The rightful candidate for office is the senior son of a senior son, but his claim may be by-passed in favour of his father's brothers or his own brothers. Since the Fulɓe are today such a small minority (1 in 20 of the population) in Gwandu Emirate and since also they live in a village area for only a part of the year, they form a group which Village Heads can afford almost to ignore. A Village Head, as a matter of practical politics, must count on the support of the majority. Then, too, because of their seasonal movements the pastoralists are not regarded by the Haaɓe as regular members of a village community. It is well known that should pastures deteriorate, political conditions become unpleasant, or for any one of many other reasons, Fulɓe quickly seek a remedy in flight. For practically any pastoralist any given village area is of interest to him only in so far as it meets a temporary need for a period which may vary from several days to a few months. But he never has the same sentimental, social, political, and economic attachment to a given village area as does a Kaaɗo. Although they may reside in a village area for a period of several months Fulɓe are always aware of the general living conditions (political, ecological, &c.) in at least several other village areas. In contrast the life of the Haaɓe men is primarily bound up in the village of their birth and with secondary ties and contacts with people in one or more contiguous villages. Haaɓe enjoy a maximum of status only if they reside with their nearest patrikin in the village of their birth—their influence and prestige is limited should they live elsewhere.

They have a degree of pride in their home and a sense of solidarity on the level of the village community which derives from kinship, common residence and more or less similar interests. Strangers, matrilateral kin, and affines suffer a limitation of status in a village throughout their lifetime.

Normally a District Head permits his Village Head to continue in office so long as he enjoys the support of his village fellows and satisfactorily carries out Native Administration instructions. For Village Heads are officials of the Native Administration, their salary varies according to the revenue of their village area, just as their responsibilities vary in proportion to the size of the village. One of their most important duties is the assessment and collection of head-tax from the Haaɓe. Normally they also assess the tax on cattle in their area, but this collection is usually done under the supervision of the District Head. A Village Head is required to carry out instructions with regard to preserving sanitary standards and providing labour for public work such as the maintenance of roads. He is expected to reconcile disputes and to report indictable offences to the District Head. The tactics used by a Village Head to gain obedience and co-operation depend upon his personality, the degree to which he enjoys popular support, and the size of the village community.

Fulɓe always come under the authority of the Village Head in whose area they are resident. Should they cause crop damage it is to him that they are answerable. If they are in his area during the tax-season (July to November) they must co-operate in assessment and make arrangements for payment. In brief, he is their link with the Native Administration. Instructions, for example, from the Veterinary Department as to quarantine of herds given through the Village Head, should be observed.

Legally the pastoralists can graze their cattle on any land which does not have a standing crop. They can also approach any Village Head to obtain permission to farm land in his area and this he cannot refuse, since upland farm-land used in growing bulrush millet (the principal crop of farming pastoralists) is not in short supply.

Although the Village Head is an official in the Native Authority—the State organization—he normally has some difficulty in exercising his authority over the Fulɓe because the village area is comparatively small and they can, as we have seen, escape by flight. It is to a Village Head's advantage to keep the herd-owners in his area, especially in the tax-season, since both his and the District Head's salary are related to the village and district revenues. However, despite the advantage of having herds within the village and district areas, there is little attempt on either level to provide adequate defined trails for cattle movement or to discourage the Haaɓe from burning grass-lands—in other words, to avoid Fulɓe-Haaɓe conflicts. But as there is sufficient pressure on grazing lands, so that if some herds move off others will come in to take their place, Village and District Heads can afford, more or less, to ignore pastoral problems since it is, as has been noted, from the much more numerous Haaɓe section of the population that they derive their support, and the Haaɓe are a group whose views, as we have seen, are antipathetic to the Fulɓe.

Because many new villages have been founded since the pacification most Village Heads are Haaɓe. And even in those Fulɓe Village Headships which have been continued since the 'Time of War', few of the present office-holders still have cattle and of these, with few exceptions, the pastoralists say, 'they have become Haaɓe'; for in gaining the support of the latter they have lost the respect of the former. The herdsmen feel that in the present century the Administration has fallen entirely into the hands of the Haaɓe and that this condition has been tacitly accepted by the British. The Fulɓe are not, as a minority with special interests, a vocal group. The fact that today the pasture-lands have been broken up by farming on a larger scale than in the pre-Protectorate period— owing to increase of population and of cash crops, mainly groundnuts—has meant that there can no longer be large local aggregates of Fulɓe. Under these conditions the most efficient basic unit is the one which the herdsmen have—the family household. This viable and mobile unit can best graze its herd on comparatively small tracts of pasture. Because of its mobility its most effective defence against the exactions of the Village Head, District Head, or *alkali* is flight; each household head sees himself as being individually pitted against these officials all of whom, having the backing of the State organization and the British, are 'stronger' than he.

It has been noted above that the Fulɓe–Haaɓe relationship is symbiotic. Indeed, it is for this reason that such a small unit as the family household can maintain its viability—or, more correctly, its independence of other pastoral households. Economic interdependence between individual pastoral households and the Haaɓe in

general is infinitely greater than between any two pastoral households. By comparison with cattle-owning peoples of East Africa,
for example, the Fulɓe are extremely specialized occupationally.
Theirs is a dairy industry. They rely on the sale of milk to the
Haaɓe for their staple food which is corn—not milk. When cattle
are sold in order to buy corn it is regarded as an irregular and
emergency measure[1] which any household head views with grave
concern. Old and diseased animals and non-serving bulls are sold
to meet occasional emergency expenses such as marriage, cattle-
tax, purchase of clothing, household equipment and medicine,
and fines. Such animals may also be sold to pay wage-labour for
farming and the building of storage bins for corn. Fulɓe pride
themselves on being inept in both these skills.

If we consider their usual material possessions it will be seen how
heavily the Fulɓe depend today upon goods purchased in the markets.

Purchased in the Markets	*Produced Domestically*[2]
Household Equipment	
Calabashes	Sleeping mats (men)
Mortar and pestle	Ropes (men)
Water pots (and cooking)	
Bottle gourds	
Spoons and ladles	
Sleeping platforms	
Knives, hoes, and axes	
Needles	
Spindle whorl	
Fire striker and flint	
Clothing	
Cloths	Spun cotton (women)
Undertrousers	
Robes	
Turbans	
Fezzes and straw hats	
Head-cloths	
Sandals	

[1] Fulɓe consume their own stock on ceremonial occasions only, namely: first
marriage, name-giving ceremony (*buki*) and, less frequently, Ramadan. Professional Haaɓe butchers are hired for slaughtering and flaying.

[2] For sleeping mats and ropes men collect their own raw materials from the
countryside when available. But raw cotton is purchased in the markets as are
often some of the ingredients for the medicines.

Purchased in the Markets	Produced Domestically
Food, &c.	
Corn	*Gero*
Rice (rare)	Milk
Meat and fish	Butter
Spices	Meat (only ceremonially con-
Salt (for human and bovine con- sumption)	sumed)
Delicacies	
Kola-nuts	
Tobacco	
Miscellaneous	
Medicines, amulets, charms	Medicine, cattle (men)
Beads, bangles, rings, &c.	Medicine, human (men and
Raw cotton	women for social and 'clinical'
Henna, kohl, scent, and soap	purposes)
Swords, daggers, spears, bows, arrows (poison), saddlery (rare)	

It will readily be seen that the Fulɓe are not accomplished in arts and crafts; practically all the items they consume and use are acquired through markets. Of course not all the items are of the same importance in their lives—some of them they can go without for shorter or longer periods or altogether. But the list does show how important trade is in their economy.

Market relations between buyer and seller tend to be very impersonal because, for both social and economic reasons, pastoralists prefer to frequent large markets. Markets visited by 1,000 to an estimated 10,000 Fulɓe and Haaɓe are normally held at least several times a week within 15 miles (the day-return limit) of any homestead. In order to make special purchases (or for other reasons) men may, if the domestic labour force permits, visit markets at twice this distance and stay over-night. Women also prefer the larger markets because milk and butter are a sort of luxury and those who can afford them are likely to be found in greater numbers at these markets. In addition, because milk is a good restorative a considerable quantity is sold to weary travellers. Some may even be sold on the road to an important market and thus lighten a woman's burden.

Almost all transactions are made in cash. This is an advantage to a woman because the values of milk and corn may vary from market to market. A clever woman may thus be able to sell milk at a comparatively high price and buy corn at a relatively low price elsewhere. A man permits his wife to attend whichever market she chooses—often they may visit the same market on the same day, but by no means always.

The market attendance habits of the Fulɓe and the Haaɓe differ. Quite apart from their having different economic interests, their social interests are dissimilar. One would be wrong in assuming that Fulɓe spend each day in the village of the village area where their homestead is located. This would happen only if the village were large, for large villages attract visitors every day and a number of transactions take place. Despite the fact that herdsmen say, 'it is nice to sleep beside the cattle', in point of fact they are lonely in the camps. Unless other interests take them elsewhere men visit the market at which they feel they will meet the most Fulɓe. Women visit the market at which they feel that they will strike the best bargain in trade. These may or may not coincide. In contrast the Haaɓe, living in villages, have a less lonely social life, their interests are closely bound up in their village community and, because they are more self-sufficient economically, they have less incentive to attend markets. Thus there may be little social contact between the village-dwellers and the herdsmen within the village area. Moreover, as has been said, when they do visit the villages Fulɓe associate mainly with one another.

There is one context, however, in which the herdsmen come in contact with the Haaɓe of their village area. This is when the cattle are brought to manure the fields of the Haaɓe. The details of the arrangements for this practice vary considerably as does the remuneration paid to herd-owners. In a minority of cases herd-owners manure the same farms year after year, and thus come into regular relations with the Haaɓe. But more often the farms manured by a given herd (and often the village area) vary from year to year. The greatest demand for manure is around the large villages where cropping is heaviest. In the more remote areas, containing only hamlets for example, Fulɓe may not be paid at all since shifting cultivation is practised. There is thus no fixed fee. Most pastoralists are quite satisfied if the Kaaɗo provides enough corn for the herd-owner's family during the manuring and perhaps an occasional gift of kola-nuts and salt. Corn is favoured as a payment because it is felt that since Haaɓe grow corn they will be more generous with it than they would be with money. Money payment (like payment in corn) is made according to the size of the herd and the length of the stay, and, of course, the local demand. If the demand is great a proportionately large number of herds may be attracted, but in these circumstances local pastures deteriorate quickly so that the advantage of gaining income from manure is offset by inferior conditions for cattle. Thus the amount and quality of local pastures may limit the degree to which manuring can be carried out. To herd-owners the condition of pastures is the basic consideration since the fertility of their herd, all other factors being equal, is dependent upon the degree to which the nutritive needs of the cattle are met. The season for manuring varies locally according to the condition of pastures—practically all of it is done between the months of December and April.

Manuring is an activity with important sociological results if only because it brings the peasants and the herdsmen into a face-to-face relationship in a context in which they recognize their mutual dependence. It is as important to the Haaße to maintain the fertility of the soil as it is to the Fulße to gain an income without effort. Manuring provides an income without increased work and helps the family household to function as an economic unit. Without this help the pastoralists would have to farm on a larger scale and either pay wage-labour or divert the domestic labour force from the tending of cattle.

It may be argued, theoretically, that the mutual dependence of Fulße and Haaße in manuring (as well as in other economic spheres) serves to reduce the tension between the two ethnic groups caused, for example, by crop damage. It can also be argued, on the other hand, that it is precisely because of competition and conflict that the two separate societies persist, despite their comparatively close contact, and do not merge. The frequent occurrence of crop damage maintains the latent hostility between the two groups and, one might argue, helps the pastoralists to maintain their ideal of ethnic endogamy. The same hostility towards the Haaße operates to produce solidarity among the pastoralists; a solidarity which is found in some measure even when there is neither kinship nor clanship or, indeed, previous acquaintance. Their sense of comradeship is such that they feel that one of their greatest 'blessings' is to have been born to their transhumant life. The thought of losing their pastoral status through lack of cattle—and thus 'becoming Haaɓe'—fills them with horror, and enables them to endure the real hardship, in comparison with the life of the Haaɓe, of 'following' cattle.

From the foregoing outline it will be appreciated that the proximity of Haaɓe, both today and in the past, has strongly influenced the Fulɓe society.

17

INTER-FAMILY RELATIONS AND THE CLAN

THROUGHOUT this report the considerable economic independence of the family household has been stressed. That is not to say, however, that Fulɓe do not, whenever possible, prefer to form associations—co-residential groupings which we may call camps. The associations are voluntary and the fact that the households which compose them are independently viable means that the camp is a very fluid grouping. The most frequent reason given by camp members for their co-residence is that 'it is pleasant to live together'. This is, of course, an over-simplification and we must examine in more detail the reasons for joining a camp and certain of the principal features of the unit.

A 'camp' is a number of households living together, all the members of which recognize a common and generally titled leader. This description would best fit the usage of the vernacular term *wuro* (pl. *gure*). For the present purpose it is convenient to think of a 'camp' as a group consisting of more than one household, even though the term *wuro* may also be used to refer to a single household. If there are only two homesteads on a common site one of the two household heads will be referred to as the *maudo* (pl. *mauɓe*, lit. 'the big person'), for in Fulɓe theory each *wuro* must have its leader.

There are a number of different titles for camp leaders, but the differences are historically, not functionally, significant. The forebears of many pastoralists now living in Gwandu lived a few hundred miles away and in their own areas their leaders bore different titles. The titles most frequently found are: *ruga*, *'ardo*, *dikko jonwuro*, and *magaji*. These cannot be placed in a hierarchical order for they all refer to a similar order of leadership. Generally speaking another term, *lamiido* (pl. *lamiiɓe*, roughly equivalent to the Hausa *sarkin*) is used to refer to a higher order of leadership such as important Village Heads, District Heads, and Emirs.

Ideally leadership passes from senior son to senior son, but the fully legitimate heir may be by-passed in favour of the junior brother of the deceased or the junior brother of the heir apparent. For example, if a leader has two wives and the senior wife is the mother of one, the senior son, while by the junior wife he has had several sons, then the senior son of the junior wife would in all probability become the leader. However, no leader or potential leader can force his claim or command obedience, no matter how sound his genealogical qualification may be. For this reason formal statements as to the ideal features of leadership today are rather meaningless. Modern leaders have little or no authority and the Fulɓe themselves more or less sum up the position in their cliché on leadership when they say, 'it is only a name' (*ɗum inɗe tan*).

The fact that camp leadership is weak or, indeed, practically non-existent is congruent with the general social structure of the community (including the Haaɓe society) and Fulɓe ecology. Much of this will have been implicit in the foregoing discussion. It was seen, for example, how the family household can, through its relationship with the Haaɓe, survive as an economic unit. Given this economic self-sufficiency *vis-à-vis* other Fulɓe households, one might ask why, in fact, are camps formed? This question must be answered before leadership can be further discussed.

An observer visiting a rather large camp of say 10 or more homesteads (20 is about the maximum) will be impressed as a rule by its good morale in contrast with camps of fewer homesteads. There is no question, as the herdsmen say, that life in the larger camps is much more pleasant. But quite apart from companionship there are other advantages in joining a camp. Small households in particular, say a man and his wife alone or a man and his wife and one herd-boy, feel more secure in a camp even though they can and do manage their own economic affairs. In the event of illness, death, divorce, or desertion by a wife, a household head in a camp can get emergency assistance. He may be able to hire a herd-boy on a per-diem basis—usually about a shilling—or he may receive prepared food from the wife of a friend or kinsman. Moreover, a household head who is short of personnel is occupied mainly in herding and does not have the opportunity to gather information on changing natural conditions of the wider community. If he is attached to a camp he can get this information from his camp fellows, or can rely on their judgement and move with them. Household heads who are thus in a weak position can, if there are no emergencies, meet their day-to-day tasks—but they suffer an inferiority of status because of the fact that they are potentially dependent. It is a basic principle of Fulɓe social organization that, to a very large extent, the status of a household head is dependent upon the 'strength' of his household; a man who has a number of sons, whose respect and obedience he commands, and who also has sufficient cattle for his needs will have status and influence whether or not he is titled or whatever his genealogy. It is known that such a household head will expect to have a voice in camp affairs because, if local social life is unpleasant, or if he does not receive from fellow household heads of the camp the respect which he feels he deserves, he will not be reluctant to move off and it is likely that other households will move with him. Since status is thus closely linked with a man's reproduction and his herd, we may understand the urgency of a youth's desire to marry and found his own household. In the same light we may interpret a man's distress over his infertility or impotence.

A camp may thus be viewed as a group of co-residential households, the heads of which have a status ranking based primarily, though not exclusively, on their 'strength' (i.e. the size of their families and their herds). Household heads with the lowest status in the camp are those who have only infant children or none and no dependent junior brothers. Households of this type do, as we have seen, manage their own tasks, but since living in isolation would be precarious for them, they depend most heavily on the camp and have the smallest voice in its affairs. Household heads who have economically productive sons or junior brothers have time to devote themselves to a household head's proper task: gaining information (in the markets) which is of vital interest to the camp concerning the conditions of pastures in other areas, whether there is bovine disease, whether flies are present, the possibility of remunerative manuring of Haaɓe fields, the cost of corn, and so forth. Pastoral conditions change quickly, especially during periods of seasonal change, so there is always need for fresh information and sufficient experience and good judgement to interpret it wisely. Thus household heads whose herding is done by their sons or younger brothers are most influential with regard to the broader interests of the camp—its movements, political relations, and so forth. Meanwhile the younger household heads, or those who do not have herding sons or younger brothers, have to devote themselves entirely to their most pressing task—the herding of their cattle—while the heads of households more favourably situated take responsibility for the wider strategy. The reward enjoyed by household heads of the latter category is comparatively high status. Thus an important function of the camp is to guarantee the advantageous movement of herds belonging to households which are deficient from the point of view of ecological requirements.

An important feature of the camp is its seasonal variation in size and composition. It is potentially a fluid group at all times and its sense of solidarity varies. There may be a question as to a household head joining a camp, but there is never a question as to an individual's right to leave it. Only when ecological conditions are at their kindest can corporate action, as for instance in a move, be easily co-ordinated. The fact that some household heads farm on a larger scale than others means that not all members are free to move at the same time. There is no system of stock loaning on any significant scale[1] so that individuals who are deficient in stock must either suffer a further reduction in animals through sale, or increase the scale of their farming. So it is that household heads do not rely on receiving much assistance from their camp fellows and must therefore maintain their self-sufficiency. They join a camp because it is in their interest to do so, but loyalty to the camp is not sufficient to hold them should they feel they can do better elsewhere. The result of this is that camps have comparatively little solidarity, but, on the other hand, a high degree of fluidity makes them ideally suited as units to the continually altering conditions of the habitat.

Both the rules of affiliation to camps as well as the observance of those rules vary locally, seasonally, and according to circumstances. By the strictest pastoral theory all household heads in a camp should be members of a single clan. Kinship among all male members need not be and rarely is traced. A man is a member of the clan of his father and there is no provision for changing this status. Even if this rule of affiliation was observed in the past, when the endogamous clan was a territorially compact group with acknowledged grazing rights, it certainly is not today. There are certain

---

[1] There is a practice called *nanga nai* by which a man lends a cow to a special friend until it has borne a calf and the calf has been weaned at two years of age. This is a token of close friendship, but it does not happen often enough to be of economic importance.

areas in which members of a given clan dominate the local pastoral population and in these circumstances the traditional ideal is most nearly realized. Affiliation, but with limitation of status, may be granted to matrilateral and affinal relations and indeed to friends who are neither, but the clan identity of the camp is generally maintained, and its leadership controlled, by a core of agnates and fellow clansmen.

Owing to its favourable year-round pastures Gwandu (as well as Argungu) has attracted a good many 'strangers' largely from Sokoto and to a smaller extent from the French Niger. Many such Fulɓe have more or less severed effective relations with their clan and have decided to live among the herdsmen of Gwandu. When a group of such 'strangers' decide to form a camp they explain their co-residence by saying that 'only because of grass we have come together' (*gam fuɗo tan min kowri*). The household heads decide among themselves who will be their leader. This is done on the basis of such various criteria as the relative age of the household heads, their experience in the area, the size of their family households, the size of the herd, and also according to 'popularity'. The chosen leader is thenceforth and without ceremony given a title which he may or may not abandon should the group disperse. Whether or not the camp becomes more or less permanent depends upon the mutual compatibility of the members and their fortunes while they are together. They may form up as a camp each year at the same season and then disperse. A camp composed of comparative strangers in an area is in a way socially desirable since they all enjoy a more or less equal status. But in consequence they are the most fluid grouping—generally surviving only for a season. In contrast, a stranger who is accepted by a camp in which most of the members are of the same clan (of which the clan-fellows say, 'because of the clan we are together', *lenyol kam kowri min*) suffers an inferiority of status which can only be diminished through years of residence, but he also enjoys a great advantage in that if the camp is within its traditional territory its members will have a detailed knowledge of the area which will be shared with the stranger.

The greatest dispersal of households takes place during the latter part of the dry season and it is at this time that most 'camps-because-of-grass' are formed, when household heads find themselves pasturing the same area and would prefer to live together.

It sometimes happens that two household heads, usually young friends, decide to form a camp 'because of friendship' (*gam higotiraagy*). They feel that larger camps, being somewhat cumbersome, do not move sufficiently to find the best pastures and also as young men they have an inferior status in the camp of more senior household heads. Together they are equal. They tend their cattle as one herd sharing the tasks equally. The household head who is not herding is thus free to make the necessary, and pleasurable, trips to the markets. A high proportion of young men in households of this type do not farm at all, for they work on the assumption that through their greater freedom of movement and the resulting efficient herding they will be able to increase the number of their cattle. Young household heads tend to be less conservative in their husbandry and take more risks than do the more experienced herd-owners.

We have seen that today a camp leader, owing to the restricted size of the group and the autonomy claimed by its constituent household heads, is not able to exercise effective leadership, or to act as a bargaining agent with the Village or District Head. The fact that a camp leader is unable to represent his camp effectively in dealing with the Native Authority contributes further to the lack of cohesion of the camp as a unit. There are too, as has been noted, ecological reasons for household autonomy which of course militates against the formation or maintenance of cohesive camps. In the past solidarity was a function of the need for defending a large local group, and also there was a closer link between the clan head and the State. Moreover, the clan was cohesive in virtue of its joint territorial rights to pasture-lands. Today, Fulɓe are disturbed by the fact that they are not, even in proportion to their small numbers, adequately represented on the Native Authority. Until such time as they are, household heads feel that they must each maintain his autonomy so that should unscrupulous officials attempt to exploit them they can best apply what they consider to be their only defence—flight. 'Running that is its defence' (*dogal kam woni magani majum*).

INDEX

Abdullahi, 8, 12.

Administration, 49, 50, 138, 148–51, 162.

Adoption, 110.

Affines, 51, 96 n., 98–100.

Age, 61–62, 67, 70, 78, 116–17, 125, 126, 128 n.

Aged, position of, 58 n., 82, 100, 113, 114, 115, 129 n.

Age fellows (-mates), 105.

Alkali, 51, 52, 80, 128, 139, 140.

Arewa, 8 n.

Askia (Songhai king), 7, 8.

Avoidance, 99–100, 102 n.

Barrenness, 109–10.

Barth, Dr. Henry (quoted), 14.

Bawa, 10, 11.

Bello, 12.

Bergube, 59.

Birnin Kebbi, 12, 18.

Bornu, 8, 10, 11.

Bororo'en, definition of, 1–3.

British conquest, 41–47, 48, 49, 148, 149.

Brothers, relationships between, 119, 127–36.

Bulls, marriage, 85, 86, 94, 95.

Burdon, Major, quoted, 16.

Burning, of bush, 17, 39, 151.

Calves, 24, 55, 102, 103.

Camps, 24, 59, 157–62; *see also* Transhumance.

Cattle, 1–3, 15, 22, 42, 55–60, 61–67; capture of, by Kebbi, 42; 'character' of, 25; importance of, 23–28, 34, 68, 148; inheritance of, 23, 137–40; loan of, 160 n.; marriage and, 77, 78 n., 85, 86, 87, 120, 121; ownership of, 23, 74; relation of to social system, 23–28; sale of, 152; taboos connected with, 71, 94; tax and, 34, 49; *see also* Herding; Transhumance.

Children, 24–25, 26, 70, 85, 93 n., 109–10, 111, 113, 115, 124; betrothal of, 82; concubines' 47; divorce and, 106; games of, 69–70,

105; language and, 36 n.; names of, 102 n.; *see also* Herding; Marriage.

Clans, 43–45, 52–53, 79, 101 n., 157–62.

Clients, 14–15.

Climate, 17; *see also* Seasons.

Concubines, 47.

Conjugal rights, restitution of, 108.

Corn, 30, 31, 32, 36, 152, 153, 154.

Cotton, 57 n.

Courts, 51, 138.

Cousin-marriage, 53, 54, 79, 80.

Cowries, 89.

Crops, 19, 30, 31, 150.

Dallanko'en, 59.

Diet, 13, 25, 111, 112.

District Heads, Districts, 148, 149, 150, 151.

Divorce, 77, 87, 89, 106, 107–8, 114 n., 143, 145.

Drainage (by rivers), 20.

Élite, 13, 14, 147.

Endogamy, 28, 47, 79.

Erosion, 17.

Family, 23, 51, 52, 55–60, 68–83, 147–56, 157–62; creation of, 68–83; head of, 51, 60, 66, 67, 68–69; herd and, 55–67; stability of, 60.

Farming, 5, 17–18, 22, 29, 30, 31, 32, 37, 38, 55, 127, 128, 131, 148, 151, 154–5.

Father–son relationship, 103, 116–36.

Fishing, 20.

'Flight', 149, 151, 162.

Fulɓe–Haaɓe relationship, 147–56.

Fulɓe na'i, definition of, 1–3.

Fulɓe siire, definition of, 1–3.

Fulfulde language, 1, 2, 6, 36 n.; differing for men and women, 105 n.; number of speakers of, 6 n.

Futa Toro, 6.

Gifts: marriage, 84–97, 107; in childbirth, 101.

Gobir, 10, 11, 12.

Gobirawa, 8.

Grandparents, 94, 135 n.

PRINTED IN
GREAT BRITAIN
AT THE
UNIVERSITY PRESS
OXFORD
BY
CHARLES BATEY
PRINTER
TO THE
UNIVERSITY

For Product Safety Concerns and Information please contact our EU
representative GPSR@taylorandfrancis.com
Taylor & Francis Verlag GmbH, Kaufingerstraße 24, 80331 München, Germany